TRUTH WITHHELD:
A SURVIVOR'S STORY

TRUTH WITHHELD: A SURVIVOR'S STORY

James T. Tague

Why We Will Never Know the Truth About the JFK Assassination

Excel Digital Press, Inc.
Dallas, Texas

Truth Withheld: A Survivor's Story
Published by:
Excel Digital Press, Inc.
P.O. Box 703978
Dallas, Texas 75370-3978
469-892-2666
ISBN 0-9718254-7-5

First Printing: October 2003

Cover Design: Kent Robbins

DEDICATION

This book is dedicated to those who were too young to comprehend and for future generations to understand why we will never know the truth about the assassination of our 35th President, John F. Kennedy. This book is intended to give the first time reader the basic facts surrounding the assassination. Every word that I have written is based on cold hard facts and firsthand knowledge. I was in Dealey Plaza that day and witnessed the killing of President Kennedy, and I testified before the Warren Commission. You will find what I have to say to be interesting and thought provoking. This book is my words, my story. I will be challenged on some of what I have to say, and that is okay because I have the documents and the firsthand knowledge to back up every word I have written. The assassination of President Kennedy changed America from a society of trust to a society of mistrust, and you need to know why.

JAMES T. TAGUE

ACKNOWLEDGMENTS

Writing this book was quite a challenge for me. Had it not been for the following people, who graciously gave their invaluable aid, encouragement, and time, I would not have completed this work. My heartfelt thanks are extended to Arvie Lee Kennedy, Andrew Graham, Pamela Martin, Kent Robbins, Ed Sieb, and Harold Weisberg for assisting me in the time-consuming task of bringing years of research into publication.

TABLE OF CONTENTS

ABOUT THE AUTHOR

I was born on a farm at home in Plainfield, Indiana with the local doctor in attendance and was the youngest of five children. I had three brothers 21, 20, and 19 years older than me, as well as a sister 14 years older. Mother was an ex-school teacher and Dad was a farmer. My parents saw to it that I was a Cub Scout, a Boy Scout (being selected as one of two to represent our area at the National Boy Scout Jamboree), participated in the Soap Box Derby, had a paper route (won a trip to Washington D.C. for most new subscriptions), and that I had a very normal life. Dad died a couple of months before mom and dad's 60th wedding anniversary. We had land though not much money, but we were not poor. Dad's word was his bond in our community. I graduated from High School at age 17 and entered the United States Air Force. I graduated from the Air Force School of Aviation Medicine, and rose rapidly in rank. My specialty was Aviation Physiology, and I taught pilot survival at high altitude, both in the classroom and in the altitude chamber. After the Air Force I answered an ad in the paper for a job as a new car salesman because it also provided a new car. Upon being hired, the sales manager tried to teach me ways of selling that went against my upbringing. The first two weeks I did not sell a car and the sales manager called me into his office. He told me he did not think I would make it, but he would give me two more weeks. I walked out of his office and started just being myself with customers, straightforward and honest. I was soon often leading the board in new car sales and a few years later I was recognized in Time Magazine as one of the nation's top salesmen. I then became a Sales Manager, General Sales Manager, and finally a General Manager. My reputation was such that I could choose to work at only the most reputable new car dealerships in the Dallas area. The automobile business has been good to me, and I have always taken pride in treating people fair and honestly. I have worked with some very fine people in my career, honest people, and a few that have sometimes given the business a black eye.

It was just an accident that I was in Dealey Plaza at 12:30 P.M. on November 22, 1963. That I was slightly injured by a missed shot was inconsequential, but the subsequent attempt by the F.B.I. to cover up that one shot did miss, and hit the curb near my feet, is important in understanding the problems the Warren Commission was to face in their investigation. The fact that I was there at the time of the assassination of President Kennedy did cause me to write down what I had witnessed that evening and held my interest through the years. Most people who are knowledgeable of the facts of the assassination credit Harold Weisberg, who died in 2002, as being the person most knowledgeable of the facts of the assassination. Harold Weisberg and I became friends about two years after the Warren

Commission findings were published. He has been a guest in my home in Dallas, and I have been a guest in his home in Frederick, Maryland. It was Harold Weisberg who sued the United States government under the Freedom of Information Act to get the Kennedy and King assassination documents released from the F.B.I. When Harold asked me to join him in that lawsuit, I did. Besides being an eyewitness to the assassination of President Kennedy, I have done extensive research on the assassination. As well as visiting the National Archives in Washington D.C., I spent many hours in Harold's basement doing research, where he kept over 60, four-drawer filing cabinets full of these F.B.I. documents. Through the years in my spare time, I have amassed several cubic feet of information. The information I have in this book is the best information available and backed up by F.B.I. reports, government correspondence, and other documentation. I have sat silently for many years seeing over 2,000 books written about the assassination of JFK, most with good intentions but lacking in facts.

James T. Tague

NOVEMBER 22, 1963

It was a bright, sunny November day as I drove on Stemmons Expressway toward downtown Dallas. I had a luncheon date with a friend and I was running late. We had set a 12-noon appointment and it was almost 12:30; I was hoping she would not be upset. When I turned off Stemmons onto Commerce Street to go through the triple underpass to downtown Dallas I was in the far left lane. As I was about to emerge from the triple underpass, the traffic stopped in front of me in my lane. I came to a halt just short of coming out from within the underpass. I sat there in my car for a moment watching a man in front of me as he stood between his car and car door, peering to his left toward Elm Street. I remember thinking that there must have been an accident or something causing this man and the cars ahead of him to stop. I got out of my car to see what was going on and walked the three or four steps to the narrow divider between Commerce and Main Streets at the very east edge of the triple underpass.

From this point, I had a clear view of Dealey Plaza. Other than the man in front of me and the other cars stopped in my lane ahead of him, there was not another person within 100 feet. I noticed a few people on the grassy knoll and a large crowd at the intersection of Houston and Elm Streets in front of the Schoolbook Depository. I stood there wondering what was going on when a limousine emerged from this crowd and headed down Elm Street toward where I was standing. It was only at this moment that I remembered that President Kennedy was going to be in Dallas that day, and that this must be his motorcade. I remember thinking how nice that I would get to see the President this close. My thoughts were quickly broken by the pop of a firecracker and I recall thinking, "What kind of idiot would be setting off a firecracker with the President driving by? The police will get him for sure." That thought was soon interrupted by the crack of a high-powered rifle shot, and then almost immediately the crack of a second high-powered rifle shot. It was then that something stung me in the face. (See photo on page 15.) My reaction to the shots came only after hearing the last shot. I remember a danger signal flashing through my mind, a signal that said these are shots, they are coming toward me, do something to protect yourself, and I jumped behind the concrete of the triple underpass for protection from the shooting. As I turned to jump under the triple underpass, the Presidential limousine shot under the underpass near me. The shooting was over.

The next few moments are a blank. I do not remember seeing the resulting rush of the crowd toward the picket fence behind the grassy knoll. It was not until later that evening, while watching television, that I realized this crowd had rushed toward the picket fence right in front of me and I had no memory of it. My racing thoughts were interrupted by a man in a suit who came running up to me and asking, "What happened?" I replied that I did not know. I was to learn later that this man was Deputy Sheriff Buddy Walthers. Deputy Walthers and I noticed a motorcycle policeman had stopped at the north curb of Elm Street near the grassy knoll and was talking to a couple of men on the sidewalk. We crossed the street to see if they knew what had happened. As we walked up to them, one of the men was exclaiming to the motorcycle policeman "His head exploded, his head exploded!" The policeman asked this man whose head, and the man sobbed "The President's!" I will never forget Deputy Sheriff Walthers turning to the grass beside the sidewalk and kicking his toe as hard as he could into the grass several times and saying, "Damn, damn, damn." As both Deputy Walthers and I stood there stunned, trying to absorb what we had just heard, I recalled that something had stung me in the face during the shooting. My testimony to the Warren Commission would state: "I felt it at the time, but I didn't associate, didn't make any connection, and ignored it. And after this happened, or maybe the second or third shot, I couldn't tell you definitely—I made no connection. I looked around wondering what was going on, and I recall this. We got to talking, and I recall that something had stung me, and then the deputy sheriff looked up and said, 'You have blood there on your cheek.' That is when we walked back down there."

To further expand on what was not said in my Warren Commission testimony, I must add that upon hearing Deputy Walthers' statement that I had blood on my cheek, I reached up with the palm of my hand and felt my face and there were drops of blood. It was then that Deputy Walthers asked me where I had been standing during the shooting and I told him it was there where he had first came up to me. At this point we were standing on the grassy knoll side of Elm Street just a minute or two after the assassination, and already traffic was back to running at normal in Dealey Plaza as if nothing had happened. We had to wait a moment for traffic to clear on Elm Street so we could go back to where I had been standing on the narrow island between Commerce and Main Streets at the east edge of the triple underpass. We crossed Elm Street and had to wait again for traffic to clear on Main Street. As we stood on the narrow island between Elm and Main Streets, Deputy Walthers said "Look, see that mark on the curb?" There on the south dirty, gray/black curb of Main Street, close to where I had been standing, was a fresh bullet mark. It was clearly that of a missed shot. The scar on the curb was visible from a distance of three traffic lanes away. We crossed Main Street and examined the curb. We could see that the bullet had hit at the very round of the curb, at a point where the side of the curb rounds into the top of the curb. The bullet appeared to have ricocheted off the round of the curb at an angle and had scraped a small amount of cement from the curb. At the angle in which the bullet had hit and by hitting at the round of the curb, the bullet could only have ricocheted off the curb; it had not hit a flat surface. The scar on the curb was about a half inch wide and we could see it had dislodged some cement. I remember Deputy Walthers taking out his ballpoint pen, trying to draw a large circle around the bullet mark, and I recall telling him that he was going to ruin his ballpoint pen on the concrete. We lined up the bullet mark and could tell it came from the general vicinity of the Schoolbook Depository or the grassy knoll. From where I was standing near the triple underpass, the grassy knoll is only a very few degrees off a direct line to the Texas Schoolbook Depository. Deputy Walthers and I then returned to the grassy knoll side of Elm Street to where the motorcycle policeman was. A large crowd was now gathering around him. (See photo on page 16.) The next few moments were blurry, but I do remember the policeman calling in on his radio that he had one man slightly wounded by a ricochet. The Dallas Police tapes show that this radio call was made at 12:37 P.M. (See copy of the Warren Report, pg. 463, Vol. X on page 17.) I was still in disbelief and trying to absorb the last few minutes when I remembered that my car was still sitting on Commerce Street under the triple underpass and blocking traffic. All the cars that had been stopped in front of me were now gone.

I had been told they needed to get a statement from me so I headed for the downtown Police Headquarters building to give a statement. On the way to Dallas Police Headquarters, I remembered my luncheon date. As her office was on the way to the police station, I stopped for a moment to tell her what had happened. She worked at a stock brokerage firm, and it was pandemonium in her office. The phones were ringing off the wall and she waved me away, indicating that she could not talk to me. I left without being able to say anything to her about the President being killed and what I had just witnessed. As I was leaving the office building, I noticed a pay phone and called my Dad in Indiana, telling him that President Kennedy had just been killed here in Dallas. Dad replied, "Now, Jim, I am watching television. He is still alive and he is at the hospital with doctors attending to his injuries." I told my Dad, "He is dead, I know because I was there."

At Dallas Police Headquarters in downtown Dallas, I had to explain why I was there and I was directed to homicide. I waited several minutes before a detective came in and proceeded to take a statement from me. Years later I was to learn his name was Gus Rose. While Detective Rose was taking notes on a notepad, a man in handcuffs was brought into homicide amidst the noise of reporters asking questions and photographers trying to take pictures of this man. Detective Rose asked one of the policemen who had brought this man in, who he was, and the policeman answered, "This is the man who just shot and killed a policeman in Oak Cliff." The man in handcuffs was placed in the glass cubical next to me and I was excused. I would later find out on television that night that the man in handcuffs who was brought into homicide while I was giving a statement was Lee Harvey Oswald.

When I walked out of police headquarters I noticed a distinct chill in the air, and I shivered. My route back to work took me down Elm Street past the Schoolbook Depository and back through Dealey Plaza where a strange thing happened for which I have no explanation. Because of the gathering crowd, policemen were now directing traffic in and around Dealey Plaza. As I was passing back through Dealey Plaza on my way to work, one of the policemen held up his hand for me to stop, and I stopped at almost the exact spot where President Kennedy had received the fatal headshot in the middle of Elm Street that afternoon. I rolled down the window and the policeman said, "We just found a large piece of the President's skull over there by the curb. It was about six inches long." I nodded and drove on. Why this policeman had stopped me to tell me this, I do not know to this day. That evening I sat down with a pen and a spiral notebook and wrote down everything I could remember about that fateful day. I then watched television until late into the morning. There was nothing on any channel but the events of the day.

Jim Tague after the shooting (highlighted). Photo Frank Cancellare.

The grassy knoll just after the shooting. Photo Jim Murray. Copyright Richard Trask.

22	Get some men up here to cover this school depository building. It's believed the shot came from, as you see it on Elm Street, looking toward the building, it would be upper right hand corner, second window from the end.
Disp	10-4. How many do you have there?
22	I have one guy that was possibly hit by a rickashay from the bullet off the concrete and another one seen the president slump.
Disp	10-4.
137	We have a man here who says he seen him pull the weapon back through the window from Southeast corner of that depository building.
Disp	All right, do you have the building covered off?
137	No, about 3/4 of a block away from there.
Disp	All right, pull on down there.
137	10-4. I'll leave these witnesses here.
257	Do you want us to go back to Mockingbird and Cedar Springs?
290	See if you can contact 125.
125	290, I am at Parkland.
290	125, do you want us to stay on Industrial or where do you want us to go?
125	At your location right now.
2	Can you give us any information as to what happened for these people out here, evidentally they had - seriousness of it - the president involved - one is at Parkland, along with Dallas 1. We have word it is unknown - Texas Depository Store, corner of Elm and Field - officers are now surrounding and searching the building.
2	Where did this happen - at Field and Main?
Disp	At Stemmons and the Triple Underpass - 12:40 p.m.
Disp	2, there's a possibility that 6 or 7 more people may have been shot.
295	I believe the president's head was practically blown off.
303	What hospital did the President go to?
Disp	Parkland Hospital
Disp	303, where are you?

74

COMMISSION EXHIBIT 705—Continued

463

Copy of the Warren Report, p. 463 of Volume X

THE MOTORCADE

The President's motorcade consisted of 17 cars and one bus. There was a pilot car that was to travel about a quarter of a mile ahead of the motorcade. The purpose of the pilot car was to alert the motorcade of any accidents, fires, obstructions, or anything that could be detrimental along the motorcade route. Then there was the lead car; it would travel about 100 feet in front of the Presidential limousine. Behind the President's limousine would be the Secret Service car and behind it would be various dignitaries and a bus with the White House Press. The motorcade started at Love Field where the President had landed after spending the night in Fort Worth. The route from Love Field through the streets of Dallas and through downtown Dallas was uneventful, with the President being greeted by a pleasant and cheering crowd. The crowd was large, but well under control. When the President's car turned onto Elm Street in front of the Schoolbook Depository, it only needed to go through Dealey Plaza and then had a clear path on Stemmons Expressway to Market Hall, where the President was scheduled to speak.

Dallas Police Chief Jesse Curry drove the lead car. In his book JFK ASSASSINATION FILE, Chief Curry states he was traveling at a speed of approximately eight to ten miles per hour toward the underpass on Elm Street, and was about halfway between Houston Street and the triple underpass when he heard the first shot. Chief Curry remembers someone in the car saying, "Is that a firecracker?" Chief Curry also recalls the shots being fairly close together, but with a longer pause between the first and second shots.

There were police motorcycle officers riding on each side of the President's limousine, slightly to the rear of the vehicle. Motorcycle Officer Bobby Hargis was near the left rear fender when a bullet hit the President in the head. With the impact of this shot, a sheet of blood and brain tissue exploded backward from the President's head onto the motorcycle windshield and Officer Hargis. The trajectory of the shot appeared to Officer Hargis to have come from ahead and to the right of the motorcade. Accordingly, Officer Hargis parked his motorcycle and started running up the grassy knoll toward the picket fence.

In the lead car, Chief Curry heard someone in the President's car over the police radio channel saying, "Let's get out of here!" There was an immediate exchange of messages by Chief Curry and it was quickly determined that the President had been hit and a motorcycle escort was quickly formed to lead the Presidential limousine to Parkland Hospital. In the first minute Chief Curry was on the air saying "Go to the hospital, officers, Parkland Hospital, have them stand by. Get men on top of the underpass, see what has happened up there, go up on the overpass. Have Parkland stand by. I am sure it's going to take some time to get your men up there. Put every one of my men there. Notify station five to move all men available out of my department back into the railroad yards and try to determine what happened and hold everything secure until Homicide and other investigators can get in there."

INSIDE THE PRESIDENT'S LIMOUSINE

The Abraham Zapruder amateur 8mm home movie captured the reaction of the occupants of the President's limousine from a split second after the first shot was fired until the limousine went under the triple underpass. A road sign obscured the limousine at the moment the first shot hit the President. As the limousine came into view from behind the sign the President was raising his hands and forearms in a horizontal motion as if he were reacting to a sharp poke in the back, or, as most interpreted this reaction, as if he was reaching for his throat. The home movie did capture on film everything else but that first split second. What the occupants of the limousine remembered months later when they testified before the Warren Commission had variances with what was captured on film. The Warren Commission's final conclusions had variances with both the occupants and what was shown in the home movie. That there were only three shots heard does not eliminate the possibility of more than three shots owing to a silencer or a simultaneous shot. All of the testimony by the occupants of the car assumed that there were only three shots.

There were six people riding in President Kennedy's limousine when the shots were fired. Two secret service agents were in the front seat, Secret Service agent Roy Kellerman was in the passenger seat, and Secret Service agent Bill Greer was the driver. Governor and Mrs. Connally were in the middle jump seats, and the President and Jackie Kennedy were in the rear seat. Both President Kennedy and Governor Connally were on the right side, the passenger side of the car and seated to the right of their wives.

THE FIRST SHOT

Governor Connally testified before the Warren Commission about the first shot as follows: "When I heard what I thought was a shot, I heard the noise which I immediately took to be a rifle shot. I instinctively turned to my right because the sound appeared to come from over my right shoulder, and I saw nothing unusual except just people in the crowd, but I did not catch the President in the corner of my eye, and I was interested, because once I heard the shot in my own mind I identified it as a rifle shot, and I immediately—the only thought that crossed my mind was that this is an assassination attempt. So I looked, failing to see him, I was turning to look back over my left shoulder into the back seat, but I never got that far in my turn. I got about in the position I am in now facing you, looking a little bit to the left of center, and then I felt like someone had hit me in the back."

Mrs. John Connally testified about the first shot as follows: "I heard a noise, and not being an expert rifleman, I was not aware that it was a rifle. It was just a frightening noise, and it came from the right. I turned over my right shoulder and looked back, and saw the President as he had both hands at his neck. It seemed to me there was—he made no utterances, no cry. I saw no blood, no anything. It was just sort of nothing, the expression on his face, and he just sort of slumped down."

Mrs. Kennedy testified before the Commission, her testimony being short, and it was justifiably obvious that her account of the shooting was troubling and that she did not have total recall of the shooting. What Mrs. Kennedy did say was: "You know, there is always noise in a motorcade and there are always motorcycles beside us, a lot of them backfiring. So I was looking to the left. I guess there was a noise, but it didn't seem like any different noise really because there is so much noise, motorcycles and things. But then suddenly Governor Connally was yelling 'Oh, no, no, no.' I was looking this way, to the left, and I heard these terrible noises. You know. And my husband never made any sound. So I turned to the right. And all I remember is seeing my husband, he had this sort of quizzical look on his face, and his hand was up, it must have been his left hand." (At this point in her testimony Mrs. Kennedy starts talking about later, after the fatal headshot and then reverts back to the first shot). She then continues: "I remember thinking he just looked as if he had a slight headache. And then I just remember seeing that. No blood or anything."

Secret Service Agent Roy Kellerman was in the front passenger seat and he testified before the Commission about the first shot as follows: "There is a report like a firecracker, pop. And I turned my head to the right because whatever this noise was I was sure that it came from the right and perhaps into the rear, and as I turned my head to the right to view whatever it was or see whatever it was, I heard a voice from the back seat and I firmly believe it was the President's, 'My god I am hit,' and I turned around and he got his hands up here like this (indicating right hand up toward the neck?). There was enough time to verify the man was hit. So, in the same motion I came right back and grabbed the speaker and said to the driver, 'Let's get out of here, we are hit.'"

Secret Service Agent Bill Greer was driving the Presidential limousine and he testified about the first shot as follows: "When we were going down Elm Street, I heard a noise that I thought was a backfire of one of the motorcycle policemen. And I didn't—it did not effect me like anything else. I just thought that it is what it was. We had so many motorcycles around us. So I heard this noise. And I thought that is what it was." And later in his testimony Agent Greer states: "The first one didn't sink in to me, didn't give me the thought that it was a shot. I thought it was the backfire of a motorcycle."

THE SECOND AND THIRD SHOTS

Governor Connally's testimony about the second and third shots: "Then I felt like someone had hit me in the back." The Governor was then asked about the time span between the first and second shots and he continued: "A very, very brief span of time. Again my trend of thought just happened to be, I suppose along the line, I immediately thought that this—that I had been shot. I knew it when I just looked down and I was covered with blood, and the thought immediately passed through my mind that there were either two or three people involved or more in this or someone was shooting with an automatic rifle. These were just thoughts that went through my mind because of the rapidity of these two, of the first shot plus the blow that I took, and I knew I had been hit, and I immediately assumed, because of the amount of blood, and in fact, that it had passed through my chest, that I had probably been fatally hit. So I merely doubled up, and then turned to my right again and began to—I just sat there, and Mrs. Connally pulled me over to her lap. She was sitting, of course, on the jump seat, so I reclined with my head on her lap, conscious all the time, and with my eyes open. And then, of course, the third shot sounded, and I heard the shot very clearly. I heard it hit him. I heard the shot hit something, and I assumed again—it never entered my mind that it ever hit anybody but the President. I heard it hit. It was a very loud noise, just that audible, very clear. Immediately I could see on my clothes, my clothing, I could see the interior of the car which, as I recall, was a pale blue, brain tissue, which I immediately recognized, and I recall very well, on my trousers there was one chunk of brain tissue as big as almost my thumb, thumbnail, and again I did not see the President at any time either after the first, second, or third shots, but I assumed always that it was he who was hit and no one else." During his testimony Governor Connally recalled two statements made by Mrs. Kennedy after the third shot and before he lost consciousness. "They have killed my husband" and "I have his brains in my hand." Also during his testimony Governor Connally is adamant that it was the second shot that hit him, and he states "It is not conceivable to me that I could have been hit by the first bullet, and then I felt a blow from something which obviously a bullet, which I assumed was a bullet, and I never heard the second shot, didn't hear it, I didn't hear but two shots. I think I heard the first shot and the third shot."

Mrs. Connally's testimony about the second and third shots: "Then there was a second shot, and it hit John (Connally), and as he recoiled to the right, just crumpled like a wounded animal to the right, he said 'My god, they are going to kill us all.'" At that point there is more testimony about Mrs. Connally pulling her husband onto her lap and trying to comfort him. And then she continues: "The third shot that I heard I felt, it felt like spent buckshot falling all over us, and then of course, I too could see that it was matter, a brain tissue, or whatever, just human matter, all over the car and both of us."

Mrs. Kennedy's testimony was very brief out of consideration for the loss of her husband, John F. Kennedy, the President of the United States; she had no distinct memory of a second shot or a third shot. Mrs. Kennedy testified that she had no memory of climbing out of her seat and on to the trunk of the limousine to retrieve a piece of the President's skull, nor did she remember Secret Service Agent Hill running up to the rear of the Presidential limousine after the third shot and pushing her back into the seat. She also testified that she only heard two shots. Her testimony about the President's head wound was deleted.

Secret Service Agent Roy Kellerman testified that in the seconds he was on the radio talking after the first shot, "A flurry of shells came into the car." His next memory is looking back and seeing Secret Service Agent Hill on the trunk. Agent Kellerman first estimated 5 seconds between the pop of a firecracker (first shot) and the second shot and then later under intense questioning changed his testimony that there were five seconds between the first and third shots. He also attempted to clarify his statement of a flurry of shells as being two shots coming in rapid succession like bang bang. Mr. Kellerman also testified that the limousine accelerated immediately after the first shot. Agent Kellerman's testimony left much to be desired.

Secret Service Agent Bill Greer's second and third shot testimony: "And then I heard it again (shot). And I glanced over my shoulder. And I saw Governor Connally like he was starting to fall. Then I realized there was something wrong. I tramped on the accelerator, and at the same time Mr. Kellerman said to me 'Get out of here fast.' And I cannot quite remember even the other shots or noises that was. I cannot quite remember any more. I did not see anything happen behind me any more, because I was occupied with getting away." In further questioning, Mr. Greer estimated that there were three or four seconds between the first and second shots and the time between the second and third shots was almost simultaneous, one right behind the other.

The Abraham Zapruder home movie reveals many discrepancies in both of the Secret Service Agents' testimonies. The President's limousine did not immediately accelerate after the first shot, the second shot, or even after the third shot; it was slowing down and almost came to a complete stop after the third shot. The Zapruder movie does seem to back up Governor Connally's version that he was hit by a different shot than the first shot that hit President Kennedy. Nevertheless, the Warren Commission concluded that both the President and the Governor were hit by the same shot, despite the positions of the men in the limousine at the time of the first shot that would indicate that this was an impossibility. That Governor Connally testified that he only heard two shots leaves questions as to his exact recollection of the shooting sequence.

PARKLAND HOSPITAL

The trip to Parkland Hospital from Dealey Plaza at high speed had happened so quickly that, when the President's limousine arrived at the emergency entrance, no one there had any idea what had happened. There were no hospital attendants at the emergency entrance at the very moment the President's limousine arrived. The hospital had been alerted, however, that the President had been injured and was on his way to the hospital just seconds before the President's car turned into the hospital driveway, and emergency personnel were headed toward the emergency entrance when the President's limousine came to a stop. The hospital's loudspeaker was blaring out "Dr. Tom Shires STAT," as Dr. Shires was in charge of surgery at Parkland. Dr. Shires was not in the hospital, but other doctors realized from the tone of voice on the loud speaker that this was no ordinary emergency and responded.

Six minutes had passed since the shooting. Mrs. Kennedy was in the back seat bowed over her husband covering his head. Blood and gore was everywhere in the limousine, the President looked dead, there was no visible sign of respiration, and his eyes were dilated and fixed. Governor Connally was bleeding profusely and he had to be removed from the jump seat before anyone could get to the President in the back seat. Governor Connally was quickly put on a stretcher as his wife Nelly looked on. As Governor Connally was being put on a stretcher, Secret Service Agent Clint Hill was trying to speak to Mrs. Kennedy. This scene was described by Dallas Chief of Police Jesse Curry in his book JFK Assassination File and I will quote, "She just sat there holding the President's head in her lap—somehow hoping to heal it, like a little girl holds a doll, then slowly she began to bend over the

President as if to shield him from the agents and attendants. It appeared she did not want anyone to see that the back of the President's head had been blown off." Agent Hill finally got through to Mrs. Kennedy and convinced her to let go of the President. He gave Mrs. Kennedy his coat, which she wrapped around the President's head and neck. Several Secret Service agents then lifted the President out of the limousine and struggled to get his limp body onto a stretcher. While this was going on outside the emergency room entrance, a full medical staff had assembled and was ready for the Governor and the President when they were rushed into emergency. Several doctors worked in vain trying to revive the President, but it was useless. The head wound was massive, and a large part of his brain was missing.

At 1 P.M. on November 22, 1963, White House Assistant Press Secretary, Malcolm Kilduff, held a press conference at the hospital and announced that President Kennedy had died. Assistant Press Secretary Kilduff told the reporters who had quickly gathered at the hospital that the President had died of a gunshot wound to the head and Kilduff pointed his finger to the right front of his head, near his right temple, to illustrate the point of entry.

White House Assistant Press Secretary Malcom Kilduff illustrates bullet's point of entry.

After President Kennedy had been pronounced dead and Governor Connally was still in surgery on the second floor, Darrell C. Tomlinson, a senior engineer for Parkland's airconditioning services was in the elevator lobby on the ground floor near the Trauma Rooms. Mr. Tomlinson had been assigned to manually operate the elevator between the ground floor and the second floor during the emergency. At one point, Mr. Tomlinson removed a stretcher from the elevator and placed it next to another stretcher near the wall. It was assumed that the stretcher that he removed from the elevator was the one that had been used to take Governor Connally up to surgery on the second floor. The other stretcher was presumed to be the one that had been used to bring President Kennedy into the emergency room from the President's limousine. Later, while standing in the elevator lobby, Mr. Tomlinson observed a doctor or an intern push one of the stretchers away from the wall to gain access to the men's room, and then leave without putting it back. Mr. Tomlinson pushed the stretcher back against the wall, and while doing so, bumped the wall with the stretcher and a spent bullet fell to the floor. During his testimony before the Warren Commission, Mr. Tomlinson estimated the time of this event to be at about 1 P.M.; however, it had to be much later for both the President's and the Governor's stretchers to be there at that time. Mr. Tomlinson turned the bullet over to Parkland Hospital's head of security, and he handed the bullet over to Secret Service Agent Richard E. Johnson, who put the bullet into his pocket. This bullet, if it was in fact an assassin's bullet, was to later become Commission Exhibit 399, also known as "the magic bullet," a bullet that the Warren Commission determined had penetrated and gone through the bodies of two men, shattering bones in one of the men, and emerging in pristine condition.

During his testimony before the Warren Commission, the stretcher that was designated stretcher "A" was the one that was removed from the elevator and stretcher "B" was the President's stretcher. When first asked which stretcher the bullet fell from, Mr. Tomlinson replied, "I believe it was 'B' (the President's)." Mr. Tomlinson was then repeatedly asked which stretcher the bullet had fallen from, and Mr. Tomlinson repeatedly said he could not be positive. At one point during Mr. Tomlinson's testimony, Warren Commission Assistant Counsel Arlen Spector states, "Now, just before we started this deposition, before I placed you under oath and before the court reporter started to take down any questions and your answers, you and I had a brief talk, did we not?" Mr. Tomlinson answered "Yes." And Spector then said, "And we discussed in a general way the information which you have testified about, did we not?" And Mr. Tomlinson answered, "Yes, sir." Spector continues, "And at the time we started our discussion, it was your recollection at that point that the bullet came off stretcher A, was it not?" And Mr. Tomlinson replied, "B." There were many more questions asked in different ways by Spector, about which stretcher the bullet fell from, with Mr. Tomlinson stating over and over again that he could not remember or be positive about which stretcher the bullet fell from. In reading Mr. Tomlinson's entire testimony before the Warren Commission, it is clear that Mr. Tomlinson wants to say that the bullet fell from the President's stretcher and that Warren Commission Counsel Arlen Spector wanted Mr. Tomlinson to say the bullet fell from Governor Connally's stretcher, causing Mr. Tomlinson to say he could not be positive regarding from which stretcher the bullet fell. It must be noted that there is no proof that either of the stretchers were the ones that carried the President or the Governor into the emergency rooms. Miss Margaret Henchcliffe testified before the Warren Commission that after the President's body had been put into a coffin, she pushed his stretcher across the hall into a vacant room. The Warren Commission determined that the bullet fell from Governor Connally's stretcher.

In 1963, no federal law covered the assassination of a U.S. President. Murder came under Texas law and by Texas law this was murder and an autopsy should be performed in Texas. Texas authorities invoked that law, but the Secret Service and Kennedy aides were adamant that they would take the President's body back to Washington D.C. with them. Hot words were exchanged and witnesses described the debate over control of President Kennedy's body as childlike. A coffin and hearse were ordered from a local mortuary and the body of the President was soon escorted to the Presidential plane at Love Field. And once Vice President Lyndon Johnson was sworn in as our new President on that plane, he, his wife Ladybird, President Kennedy's body, Jackie Kennedy, and the Presidential entourage were flown back to Washington D.C.

THE EMERGENCY ROOM AND TRAUMA ROOM 1

What the doctors and nurses observed about the condition of President Kennedy upon his arrival at Parkland, and while they were attending to him, should have been crucial to the final findings of the Warren Commission. Many of these professionals had attended to hundreds of emergencies, including hundreds of gunshot wounds. Parkland Memorial Hospital was the primary hospital for receiving emergencies in Dallas. For some reason the Warren Commission, in its final conclusions, chose to ignore the first hand observations of these doctors and nurses, which, as we now know today, 40 years later, is a major reason why we have a controversy over what really happened in Dealey Plaza. By the time the Parkland Hospital doctors testified before the Warren Commission, they had become aware of the Autopsy Report and what it contained, a report that we now know is questionable at best, if not false. When one reads the Parkland doctors' testimonies before the Warren Commission, the influence of knowing the autopsy results comes through. It has also been acknowledged that the doctors were prepared before their testimony, as to what questions they were going to be asked. You, the reader, should read these doctors' entire Warren Commission testimony and make up your own mind as to the influence knowing the questionable autopsy results would have on their testimony. The complete 26-volume Warren report is available on the Internet.

The Parkland Hospital doctors and nurses who attended to the President were respected professionals, and these respected professionals were the first ones to see the President's injuries. Their testimony before the Warren Commission should have been taken as an absolute fact, as to what they observed, for they had nothing to gain and nothing to hide by saying otherwise. They all saw the same thing and they all testified that there was a large hole in the back of the President's head. Some spoke in medical terms, referring to the back of the head as the occipital area and using other medical terms to describe the President's head wound, but what they all testified to was a large "exit" wound in the right rear of the President's head extending up into the top of the skull with brain tissue and blood oozing from the wound. They saw a very small "entrance" wound in the throat and most of the doctors, given a set of circumstances, were made to admit that the throat wound could have been an exit wound. None of the doctors testified that they saw an entrance wound below the large exit wound in the back of the head. That same evening, the autopsy doctors, who had maybe observed one or two bullet wounds in their entire career, compared to the Parkland Hospital Emergency room doctor's observations of hundreds of bullet wounds, did not report seeing the large exit wound in the back of President Kennedy's head on their autopsy report. RN Diana Bowron was one of the first to respond. She heard over the intercom that they needed carts at the emergency room entrance and rushed a cart, along with an orderly, down the hallway to be met by what she assumed to be Secret Service agents. The Secret Service agents were encouraging them to run. When they got to the President's limousine, they had to wait while Governor Connally was removed from the car so they could get to the President. When Ms. Bowron testified before the Warren Commission, she was asked what she had observed about the President. Ms. Bowron replied, "He was moribund, he was lying across Mrs. Kennedy's knee and there seemed to be blood everywhere. When I went around to the other side of the car I saw the condition of his head." Ms. Bowron was then asked about the condition of the President's head and she replied, "The back of his head, well it was very bad, you know." Ms. Bowron is then asked how many holes she saw and she replied, "I just saw one large hole." Ms. Bowron was then asked if she saw a small bullet hole below the large hole and she replied "No." As soon as Governor Connally was removed from the limousine, Mrs. Bowron started to help lift the President's head onto the stretcher, but Mrs. Kennedy pushed her away and lifted the President's head herself onto the cart.

Margaret M. Henchcliffe was an RN who was on duty in the Parkland emergency area. Ms. Henchcliffe had spent the last seven years as an emergency room nurse and had witnessed hundreds of bullet wounds during that time. When Ms. Henchcliffe saw a stretcher being rushed through the emergency area, she helped bring the stretcher into the Trauma Room. Ms. Henchcliffe did not realize it was the President until after she was sent for blood a couple of minutes later. Ms. Henchcliffe testified before the Warren Commission that the throat wound was just a little hole and had all the characteristics of an entrance wound, that there was no blood around the little hole and it was not jagged like most of the exit wounds she had seen. Ms. Henchcliffe was not asked about the President's head wound.

Dr. Charles J. Carrico was the first Doctor at the Trauma Room to receive the President. When Dr. Carrico testified before the Warren Commission, he was asked about his initial observation of the President and he replied, "He was lying on a carriage, his respirations were slow, spasmodic, described as agonal." Dr. Carrico is interrupted and asked what he meant by agonal. Dr. Carrico replies, "These are respirations seen in one who has lost his normal coordinated central control of respiration. These are spasmodic and usually reflect a terminal patient. His—the President's color—I don't believe I said—he was an ashen, bluish, gray, cyanotic, he was making no spontaneous movements, I mean, no voluntary movements at all." Dr. Carrico went on to describe the actions taken by the doctor himself and other doctors. He described the throat injury as a rather round 4-7 mm wound with no jagged edges or stellate lacerations. Dr. Carrico, under intense questioning, did say that the neck wound could have been either an entry or an exit wound. Dr. Carrico was then asked to describe the President's head wound and the doctor replied, "The wound that I saw was a large gaping wound, located in the right occipitoparietal area." Webster's Dictionary defines the occipital bone as the bone that forms the posterior part of the skull. For us who are not doctors, Dr. Carrico was saying there was a large gaping hole in the right back side of the President's head. Dr. Carrico went on to describe the gory details of this injury in medical terms. When asked if he noticed a bullet hole below the gaping wound, Dr. Carrico replied, "No."

Dr. Malcomb O. Perry was having lunch in the main dining room with Chief Resident Dr. Ronald Jones when he was alerted by the speaker system of an emergency. Dr. Perry arrived in the Trauma Room to find Dr. Carrico at the head of the table attaching the oxygen apparatus to assist in the President's breathing. When Dr. Perry testified before the Warren Commission he was asked what he had observed about the President's condition and he replied, "I noted there was a large wound of the right posterior parietal area in the head exposing lacerated brain." Dr. Perry was again asked later in his testimony regarding what he observed as to the President's head specifically. Dr. Perry answered, "I saw no injuries other than the one which I noted to you, which was a large avulsive injury of the right occipital-parietal area." Dr. Perry was then asked if he saw a bullet hole below the large avulsed area and Dr. Perry replied, "No."

Dr. William K. Clark was in the laboratory at Southwestern Medical School, next to Parkland Hospital, when he got a call from the hospital. Dr. Clark immediately rushed to the Trauma Room. When he arrived in the Trauma Room, Dr. Perry was performing a tracheotomy on the President, and

Dr. Jones and Dr. Carrico were administering fluids and blood intravenously. Dr. Clark testified before the Warren Commission and when asked to describe what he observed regarding the President's condition, Dr. Clark described the President's general condition. Then he said about the head injury, "I then examined the wound in the back of the President's head. This was a large gaping wound in the right posterior part, with cerebral and cerebellar tissue being damaged and exposed." In layman's terms, right posterior part, is right rear of the head. Dr. Clark was asked if he observed a bullet hole in the back of the President's head and he replied, "No sir, I did not. This could have easily been hidden in the blood and hair." It is interesting to note that after Dr. Clark's testimony describing a large gaping hole in the 'back' of the President's head, Dr. Clark was then asked a question that countered what he had previously said. Dr. Clark was asked, "Now, you described the massive wound at the 'top' of the President's head, with the brain protruding; did you observe any other wound on the President's head?"

Dr. Robert N. McClelland was showing a film on surgical techniques to a group of students when he was alerted. When Dr. McClelland arrived in the Trauma Room, several other doctors were already there working on the President, and Dr. McClelland was soon positioned at the President's head helping Dr. Perry. When Dr. McClelland testified before the Warren Commission, he was asked what he had observed about the President's head injury and Dr. McClelland replied, "I was in such a position that I could very closely examine the head wound, and I noted that the right posterior portion of the skull had been extremely blasted. It had been shattered, apparently by the force of the shot, so that the parietal bone was protruded up through the scalp and seemed to be fractured almost along its right posterior half, as well as some of the occipital bone being fractured in its lateral half. And this sprung open the bones that I mentioned in such a way that you could actually look down into the skull cavity itself and see that probably a third or so, at least, of the brain tissue, posterior cerebral tissue and some of the cerebellar tissue had been blasted out." Dr. McClelland described the throat wound as less than a quarter of an inch in diameter and when he said, "We all thought it was an entrance wound," Dr. McClelland was asked what he meant by we, to which he replied, "Essentially all the doctors that have been mentioned here." With more questioning, Dr. McClelland said the throat wound could be either an entry or an exit wound, but it would be impossible to determine which. The Warren Commission determined it was an exit wound.

Dr. Charles R. Baxter was conducting the student health service when he was contacted by the supervisor of the emergency room and alerted that the President was there. Dr. Baxter testified before the Warren Commission and he was asked what he had observed about the condition of the President, to which he replied, "He was obviously in extremis. There was a large gaping wound in the skull which was covered at that time with blood, and its extent was not immediately determined." Dr. Baxter is then asked questions about the treatment of the neck wound, the tracheotomy, when the priest arrived, time of death, efforts made, what doctors present, and then asked again about the head wound, being requested to describe in as much particularity as he could the nature of the head wound. Dr. Baxter answered, "The only wound that I actually saw—Dr. Clark examined this above the manubrium, the sternum, the sternal notch. This wound was in temporal parietal plate of bone laid outward to the side and there was a large area, oh, I would say 6 by 8 or 10 cm of lacerated brain oozing from this wound, part of which was on the table and made a rather massive blood loss mixed with it and around it." Dr Baxter's description of the head injury was a little different than the other doctors and nurses and it put the massive head injury at the top of the head, but Dr. Baxter had already said, "Its extent was not immediately determined." Was Dr. Baxter trying to say with this statement that he did not get a good look at the wound? There were more questions about the neck wound, and Dr. Baxter stated the wound was more compatible with an entry wound than an exit wound. When asked, Dr. Baxter stated that he had been at Parkland Hospital for six years and "We admit and treat, I would estimate, around 500 gunshot wounds per year—thereabouts." He was then asked if he had any formal training in gunshot wounds.

Dr. Marion T. Jenkins was in the dining room when he heard the Chief of Surgery, Dr. Tom Shires being paged "stat." Dr. Jenkins knew Dr. Shires was out of town and that "stat" meant emergency, and that something bad had happened. Dr. Ronald Jones was with Dr. Jenkins and Dr. Jones answered the page. Dr Jones hung up the phone, and with an anguished look, the color drained from his face, said, "The President has been shot and is on the way to the hospital." At the same moment, they heard the sirens of the police motorcycles as they turned into the emergency entrance driveway. They knew this was the President because ambulances always turned off their sirens before entering the driveway. Dr. Jenkins raced upstairs and notified two associates of the situation and then raced to the Trauma Room. Dr. Jenkins was an anesthesiologist and his testimony gave great detail as to what was being done to the President—who was there, who was doing what, and so on. In reading his testimony, it is obvious that he was also too busy with his duties in this emergency to have examined President Kennedy's head wound. Why Dr. Jenkins did not just say that he did not get a good look at the President's head wound, I do not know, but it is typical of so many witnesses that when pressed for an answer by being asked the same question in different ways, they finally answer to please the Counsel asking the questions. That Arlen Spector, Assistant counsel for the Warren Commission, uses the autopsy report as a reference point for the Parkland doctors in their testimony is wrong. Dr. Jenkins testified before the Warren Commission, and when first asked about what he had observed concerning the condition of the President, he described everything in great detail except the head wound. Dr. Jenkins was asked other questions and then once more asked about the head wound. He again skirted a direct description of the injury. Dr. Jenkins was then, for the third time, asked about the head wound and he replied, "I don't know whether this is right or not, but I thought there was a wound on the left temporal area, right in the hairline and right above the zygomatic process." Dr. Jenkins was told by Arlen Spector, "The autopsy report discloses no such development, Dr. Jenkins."

Dr. Ronald C. Jones was a resident surgeon at Parkland Hospital. He was eating lunch with Dr. Perry when he heard the page for Dr. Shires "stat." Dr. Jones was one of the first doctors to arrive at the Trauma Room. During his tenure at Parkland, Dr. Jones spent many hours in the emergency room, sometimes attending to as many as four or five bullet wounds a night. When Dr. Jones testified before the Warren Commission, he was asked if he had observed any wounds and he replied, "As we saw him the first time, we noticed that he had a small wound at the midline of the neck, just above the superasternal notch, and this was probably no greater than a quarter of an inch in greatest diameter, and that he had a large wound in the right posterior side of the head." Dr. Jones was then asked to describe in detail the head wound and he answered, "There was a large defect in the back side of the head as the President lay on the cart with what appeared to be some brain hanging out of this wound with multiple pieces of skull noted next with the brain and with a tremendous amount of clot and brain." Dr. Jones is then read a report he had made of his activity in the Trauma Room that day. In that report, he noted about the neck wound, "A small hole in the anterior midline of the neck thought to be a bullet entrance wound." Dr. Jones was asked to explain this statement, and he replies, "The hole was very small and relatively clean cut, as you would see in a bullet that is entering rather than exiting from a patient. If this were an exit wound, you would think that it exited at a very low velocity to produce no more damage than this had done, and if this were a missile of high velocity, you would expect more of an explosive type of exit wound, with more tissue destruction than this appeared to have on superficial examination." Dr. Jones is then asked if he had any experience with a throat wound inflicted by 6.5 bullet? Dr. Jones replied "No, not to the throat, but to other parts of the body." Dr. Jones also stated in his testimony, that the large hole in the back of the President's head appeared to be an exit wound.

Dr. Gene C. Akin was notified while on duty in the operating suite that anesthetic assistance was needed in the emergency room. When Dr. Akin testified before the Warren Commission, he was asked what he had observed about the head wound and he answered, "The back of the right occipital-parietal portion of his head was shattered, with brain substance extruding." When Dr. Akin was asked if he had an opinion about the direction of the headshot, he replied, "I assume that the right occipitalparietal region was the exit, so to speak, that he had probably been hit on the other side of the head, or at least tangentially in the back of the head, but I did not have any hard and fast opinions about that either."

Dr. Paul C. Peters was preparing lecture material for medical students and went to the emergency room to see if he could be of any assistance. Dr. Peters testified before the Warren Commission, and when asked about the head wound he replied, "And as I remembered—I noticed that there was a large defect in the occiput." Dr. Peters was asked what he noticed in the occiput, and he answered, "It seemed to me that in the right occipital-parietal area that there was a large defect. There appeared to be brain loss and bone loss in the area." Dr. Peters did say in his testimony that the doctors speculated that the neck wound was an entry wound and the wound in the back of the head was an exit wound.

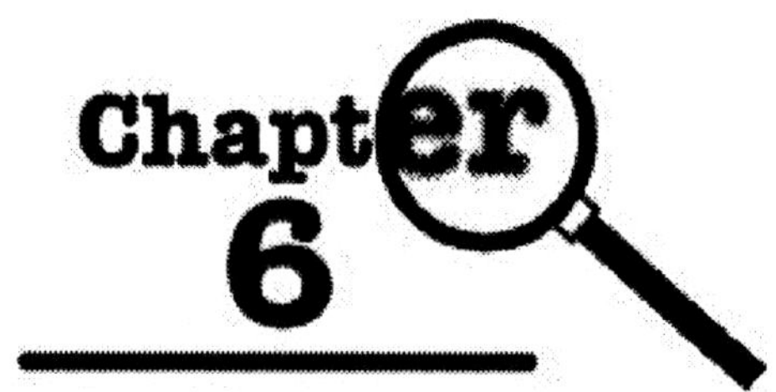

THE EMERGENCY ROOM, TRAUMA ROOM 2 AND SURGERY

Governor John Connally had to be removed from the Presidential limousine first, since he was in the middle jump seat and preventing access to the President in the rear seat. The Governor was conscious and his coat and shirt were covered with blood in front. He was rushed into the emergency area and into Trauma Room 2, where IV's and other medical procedures were started and the Governor was stripped of his clothing. A preliminary examination found a sucking chest wound and a tube was inserted to expand the Governor's right lung. Governor Connally was complaining bitterly about the pain. About 12 minutes had elapsed when several doctors took the Governor from the ground floor Trauma Room to the second floor for surgery. Just outside the operating room the Governor was removed from his stretcher and placed on an operating table and then pushed into the operating room for surgery. Governor Connally was soon to be in the hands of two of the most talented and capable surgeons in the United States, both having had extensive battlefield and civilian gunshot wound experience.

Dr. Robert R. Shaw had been at a conference and was on his way back to the hospital when he stopped for a traffic light near the hospital. As he was stopped at the light, the President's car came speeding by with a police escort on the way to the hospital. Dr. Shaw also heard on his car radio at about the same time that the President had been shot. He stopped at The Children's Hospital next to Parkland Hospital, where he learned that Governor Connally had also been wounded. Dr. Shaw walked the 150 yards to the Parkland Hospital Emergency area and entered Trauma Room 2, where Governor Connally was being attended.

Dr. Shaw was a certified Thoracic (chest) Surgeon. During and after WW II, Dr. Shaw had served as chief of the thoracic surgery center in Paris, France. Dr. Shaw testified to the Warren Commission that the center had attended to over 900 chest wounds, many of them bullet wounds. He also testified that he had experience with over 1,000 bullet wounds to the chest. Dr. Shaw's testimony before the Warren Commission was first taken on March 23, 1964. Assistant Warren Commission Counsel Arlen Spector took Dr. Shaw's testimony, and the questions and answers about Governor Connally's chest wound got sidetracked with questions and answers about the wrist wound and which side of the wrist was entry or exit. There were many off-the-record conferences. Dr. Shaw did state in his March 23 testimony that there were no bullet fragments found in Governor Connally's chest. Dr. Shaw was recalled to testify again on April 21, 1964. (I will start with testimony that begins in the operating room.) Governor Connally was given anesthesia by Dr. Giesecke. Dr. Shaw recognized the wound below the right nipple as an exit wound owing to its size and jagged edges. Once fully anesthetized, Governor Connally was rolled over and the back wound was examined. It was a small wound, had clean cut edges, was an entrance wound, was roughly elliptical, was located even with the right armpit on the far right side of the back, and the bullet had missed the shoulder blade. At this time, Dr. Shaw had not discovered the thigh wound and Dr. Shaw assigned the treatment of the wrist wound to Dr. Gregory. During the chest operation, Dr. Shaw discovered that the fifth rib had been hit by a bullet and was shattered, and that fragments of bone had to be removed. Dr. Shaw also testified that the rib at this point was not of great density, but could cause a slight deflection of the bullet. In his testimony before the Warren Commission, Dr. Shaw then goes into great detail in medical terminology to describe the damage to the lung tissue and muscle tissues that the bullet had caused, and the required repairs. Dr. Shaw is shown the pristine bullet that was retrieved from the floor at Parkland Hospital, now known as Commission Exhibit 399. Dr. Shaw is then asked if this pristine bullet, Commission Exhibit 399, could have caused all three of Governor Connally's wounds, wounds to the chest, wrist, and thigh. Dr. Shaw answered, "I feel there would be some difficulty in explaining all of the wounds as being inflicted by bullet Exhibit 399 without causing more in the way of loss of substance to the bullet or deformation of the bullet." The Commission hearing then goes off the record. When the hearing resumes, Dr. Shaw is shown the Zapruder movie and asked if he can pinpoint the frame that the Governor is hit, in relation to the Governor's injuries. Dr. Shaw states, "Frame 236, give or take 1 or 2 frames." Dr. Shaw is then asked if he has an "opinion" about the possibility that one bullet hit both the President and the Governor. Dr Shaw replied, "Yes. From the pictures, from the conversation with Governor Connally and Mrs. Connally, it seems that the first bullet hit the President in the shoulder and perforated the neck, but this was not the bullet that Governor Connally feels hit him; and in the sequence of films, I think it is hard to say that the first bullet hit both of these men almost simultaneously." Dr. Shaw is asked if a person could have a delayed reaction to sensing that they have been hit by a bullet and the doctor responded, "Yes, but when the bullet strikes bone, the reaction is usually quite prompt."

Dr. Charles F. Gregory was an orthopedic surgeon who served in the Navy during WW II, and in the Korean War in support of the First Marine Corps division. When asked by the Warren Commission Counsel how many bullet wounds he had treated, he estimated he had dealt directly with 500 such wounds. Dr. Gregory was seeing patients at the hospital at the time the President and the Governor were admitted. He first checked emergency to see if his services were needed with the President and was told they were not needed. He then prepared to leave the hospital, but stopped by the surgical suite on the way out and encountered Dr. Shaw. Dr. Shaw retained Dr. Gregory to treat Governor Connally's wrist injury. Once Dr. Shaw had attended to the Governor's chest wounds, Dr. Gregory examined the Governor's wrist and thigh wounds. Dr. Gregory found an entry wound on the top of the wrist and an exit wound on the palm side of the wrist about an inch above the fold of the wrist. The entry wound was about half a centimeter by two and one half centimeters and the exit wound was about a half a centimeter by two centimeters. The entry wound was larger than the exit wound and, in Dr. Gregory's opinion, the entry wound was caused by an irregular object. Dr. Gregory testified about the shattered bones above the wrist and that the x-rays showed at least seven bullet fragments, which the doctor pointed out to the Commission. The three largest metallic fragments varied from five-tenths of a millimeter in diameter to approximately two millimeters in diameter and no more than a half-millimeter in thickness. They were metal flakes. Dr. Gregory also found cloth fragments in the wound similar to Governor Connally's coat fabric. Two of the bullet fragments were removed and given to a nurse, who in turn gave them to a Texas Ranger. During Dr. Gregory's testimony, he was shown the bullet that was found on the floor at Parkland Hospital, Commission Exhibit 399, and was asked if that bullet could have caused the wounds to Governor Connally's wrist. Dr. Gregory examined the pristine bullet and answered, "I find a small flake has been either knocked off or removed from the rounded end of the missile, I was told this was removed for analyses, the only other deformity which I find is at the base of the missile at the point where it joined the cartridge carrying the powder, I presume, and this is somewhat flattened and deflected, distorted. There is some irregularity of the darker metal within which I presume to represent lead. The only way this missile could have produced this wound, in my view, was to enter the wrist backward." Dr. Gregory was then asked if this pristine bullet had enough lead missing to account for the lead found in Governor Connally's wrist and Dr. Gregory replied that he did not know enough about this particular bullet to know what was normal. Senator Russell asked Dr. Gregory when he had first seen Commission Exhibit 399, and the doctor replied, "This morning." Dr. Gregory was then asked about the thigh wound and the doctor described the wound as being about a third up the leg from the knee and on the inside of the leg and that it was a puncture wound about the size of an eraser. Dr. Gregory was asked if one bullet could have caused all three of Governor Connally's wounds and the doctor answered that the three wounds to the Governor could have occurred from one bullet. Dr. Gregory was then asked if one bullet could have caused all the wounds in both President Kennedy and Governor Connally, and Dr. Gregory answered, "I believe one would have to concede the possibility, <u>but I believe firmly that the possibility is much diminished</u>." The doctor was then asked why he had said that, and the doctor replied, "I think that to pass through the soft tissues of the President would have certainly decelerated the missile to some extent. Having then struck the Governor and shattered a rib, it is further decelerated, yet it has presumably retained sufficient energy to smash the radius. Moreover, it escaped the forearm to penetrate at least the skin and fascia of the thigh, <u>I am not persuaded that this is very probable</u>. I would have to yield to possibility."

THE SCHOOLBOOK DEPOSITORY

The Texas Schoolbook Depository was just that, a storage building for textbooks. It was seven stories tall and was located on the northwest corner of Elm and Houston Streets, at the very west end of downtown Dallas. On November 22, 1963, Roy Truly was the depository superintendent. On October 15, 1963, five weeks before the assassination of President Kennedy, Mr. Truly received a call from a Mrs. Paine, a woman who lived in Irving. She was inquiring about employment for a man named Lee Harvey Oswald. After a brief conversation, Mr. Truly told her to send Mr. Oswald in to fill out an employment application. Lee did come in and filled out an employment application and was hired to be a schoolbook order filler and went to work the next day. Lee seemed grateful to be hired and he quickly learned his job, mostly working on the first and sixth floors. Mr. Truly would greet Lee in the morning with "Good morning, Lee," and Lee would reply "Good morning, sir." If Mr. Truly would ask Lee about his new baby, Lee would always give Mr. Truly a big smile.

On November 22, 1963, Roy Truly was going to lunch at about 12:15 P.M. with O. V. Campbell, who was Vice President of the depository. As they went out the front door, they noticed the crowd that had gathered in front of the depository to watch President Kennedy's motorcade, and they decided to wait for the motorcade themselves. When the President's limousine made the turn off Houston Street on to Elm, the limousine made too wide of a turn and almost ran over the curb where they were standing. Immediately after the third shot, the crowd surged back from the street in terror or panic, forcing Mr. Truly almost back to the steps of the depository building. At that moment, Roy Truly saw a young motorcycle policeman run right by him, rushing through the crowd and pushing people aside as he ran up to the front entrance to the depository. The policeman was Marrion L. Baker who had been riding beside one of the press cars four or five cars behind the President's limousine. In this position in the motorcade, Officer Baker had not yet turned off Houston Street onto Elm and was facing the front of the Schoolbook Depository when the shooting started. Mr. Truly ran after the policeman and caught up with him in the lobby of the building. Truly's thoughts were that the policeman wanted to get to the roof and he needed to show him the way. They ran for the elevators, but the elevators were on an upper floor. The policeman then asked Mr. Truly where the stairway was and they ran to the stairs and started up the stairs with Truly leading the way. On the second floor, Baker saw a man in the lunchroom out of the corner of his eye. Truly had gone up three or four more steps when he realized the policeman was no longer behind him, so he stopped and returned to the second floor landing. Baker had drawn his gun and had the gun aimed at Lee Oswald. Baker asked Roy Truly if the man worked there, and Truly replied "Yes." Oswald then casually walked over to the coke machine and bought a coke. Roy Truly and Officer Baker then continued up the stairs.

In his testimony before the Warren Commission, Officer Baker testified that when he encountered Oswald in the lunchroom, Oswald did not seem to be out of breath and appeared normal, calm, and collected. In two trial runs to reenact Officer Baker's movements from the time of the first shot until he encountered Oswald in the lunchroom, the time was a minute and 30 seconds on the first trial run and a minute and 15 seconds on the second trial run. Officer Baker also participated with Secret Service Agent John Howlett in timing how long it would take for someone to go from the sniper's nest on the sixth floor, down the stairs, and into the lunch room on the second floor. At a normal walk, it took a minute and 18 seconds. At a fast walk, it took a minute and 14 seconds.

Bonnie Ray Williams was helping to re-floor the upper floors of the depository. On November 22, 1963, he had taken a position on the fifth floor to watch the President's motorcade. His position was almost under the sixth floor window from which the shots were fired. He testified that the shots shook the building so hard that dirt or debris fell from the ceiling, and that the shots came from over his head, from the floor above him.

James Jarmon Jr. was an order checker for the Depository. On November 22, 1963, Mr. Jarmon had taken a position near Bonnie Ray Williams on the fifth floor to watch the motorcade. He had raised a window to get a better view and was on his knees watching the motorcade when the shots were fired. He too thought the shots came from inside the depository. He also noticed white dust, like plaster, in Mr. Williams' hair after the shooting. Mr. Jarmon made a statement in his testimony to the Warren Commission that makes one pause for thought. Mr. Jarmon testified that earlier he had been on the first floor talking to Oswald and I quote, "Well, he (Oswald) was standing up in the window and I went to the window also, and he asked me what were the people gathering around on the corner for, and I told him that the President was supposed to pass that morning, and he asked me did I know which way he was coming, and I told him yes, he would probably come down Main and turn on Houston and then back again on Elm." Oswald then replied, "Oh, I see" and that was all.

Harold Norman was an order filler at the depository. On November 22, 1963, Norman was on the fifth floor near Williams and Jarmon and had also raised a window to watch the motorcade when the shots were fired. He testified before the Warren Commission that he heard the shell hulls hitting the floor above him and the ejecting of the rifle when the shots were fired. He also noticed white dust in Williams' hair after the shooting.

Charles Givens was also a book handler at the Depository. On the afternoon of the assassination, Givens gave a statement to the F.B.I. that he had seen Oswald in the Domino Room on the first floor, reading a newspaper at 11:50 A.M. Three other depository employees also saw Oswald in the Domino Room at this time. Givens would later change his statement when his testimony was taken in secret by David Belin of the Warren Commission.

At 12:36 P.M., Sergeant D. V. Harkness radioed in that he had a witness that said the shots came from the fifth floor. The witness was Amos Lee Euins, a 15-year-old spectator, who recalled that just before the shots were fired he saw "this pipe thing sticking out the window." After the first shot he looked up and saw a rifle with a hand on the barrel and another hand on the trigger sticking out the open window. Euins identified the fifth floor as the floor under the ledge, which would have actually been the sixth floor.

Mr. and Mrs. Arnold Rowland were spectators standing across the street from the Depository. A few minutes before the shooting, Arnold looked up and saw two men standing together in the sixth floor corner window of the Depository, and one was holding a rifle. Arnold Rowland assumed these were agents assigned to protect the President. When Mr. Rowland looked back up to the window a minute or so later, "The other man was gone, and there was just one man, the man with the rifle." Deputy Sheriff Roger D. Craig referred Mr. and Mrs. Rowland to F.B.I. agents who interviewed them. No statement can be found in any F.B.I. report about a second man or of an accomplice.

Howard I. Brennan was standing across the street from the depository and heard the first shot, and he looked up and saw the sniper fire a second shot. That evening, November 22, 1963, Howard Brennan watched a police lineup with Oswald being one of the men in the lineup. Mr. Brennan could not positively identify Lee Harvey Oswald as the shooter he saw in the window. Mr. Brennan's statements to the F.B.I. varied from month to month after the assassination, and by the time he testified before the Warren Commission, he positively identified Lee Harvey Oswald as the man he saw in the window of the Schoolbook depository from 125 feet away.

Other bystanders saw the rifle as it was withdrawn from the sixth floor window. It took seven or more minutes for the police to coordinate these scattered witness reports and determine that shots had been fired from the Schoolbook Depository, and then to seal off the building. With the help of building Superintendent Roy Truly, each employee of the building was checked off and sent home; Lee Harvey Oswald was the only one missing. The building was then searched from top to bottom. Three spent shell casings were found near the corner window on the sixth floor, and a partially hidden rifle was found near the stairwell. The rifle was traced to O. H. Hidel. When arrested, Lee Harvey Oswald had an identification card with the name O. H. Hidel on it.

When Roy Truly testified before the Warren Commission, he was asked about Oswald's demeanor when encountered in the lunchroom a minute after the assassination, and Truly replied, "He didn't seem to be excited, or overly afraid or anything. He might have been a little bit startled like I might have been if somebody confronted me. But I cannot recall any change in expression of any kind on his face."

There is no question that the evidence points directly to Lee Harvey Oswald as the assassin, or at least as a co-conspirator, in the assassination of President John F. Kennedy and the wounding of Governor John Connally. That Oswald could calmly be reading a newspaper 40 minutes before he murdered President Kennedy and be calm and collected a minute after the assassination still bothers me 40 years later. I cannot imagine such calm behavior before and after the assassination of the most powerful man in the world. I also find it intriguing that Oswald would ask why people were standing around at the corner and have to be told that the President was going to be passing by.

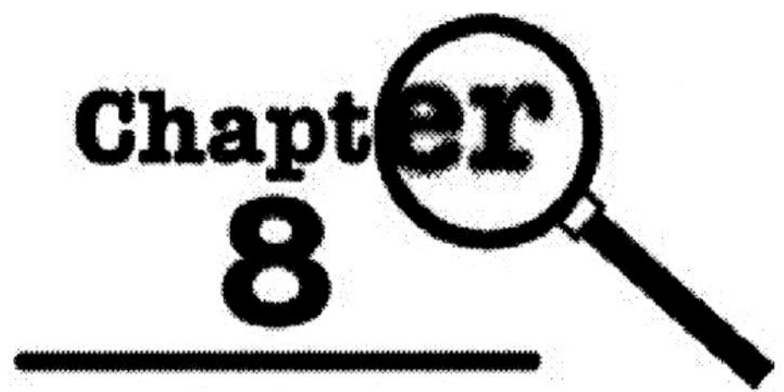

BEHIND THE FENCE

The Abraham Zapruder home movie clearly shows President Kennedy's head being violently thrown back so hard that the momentum of the President's head also throws his shoulders and body into the back of the seat. These film clips clearly indicate the distinct probability that at least one shot came from the front. Through the years there have been many theories advanced as to why his head would react opposite and contrary to all laws of physics. Two of these theories are a "neuro-reaction" and a "jet effect." These theories are yet to be proven by experts on physics. When you hit something with any object, the energy expended in hitting the object causes the object to go away from the impact of the hit. I have yet to meet a hunter that has had an animal react toward the shooter after being shot. The power and energy of the bullet hitting the animal knocks the animal away from the shooter. Thus, with the President's head and shoulders being violently thrown back into the seat, there is the probability that at least one shot came from in front of the President, which threw him away from the source of the shot. There were credible witnesses on the triple underpass and elsewhere whose statements and testimony suggest that the source of a frontal shot was from behind and over the picket fence at the rear of the grassy knoll.

Motorcycle policeman Bobby Hargis was riding his motorcycle at the left rear of the President's car when the fatal headshot hit President Kennedy. I will quote from his Warren Commission testimony: "It seemed like his head exploded, and I was splattered with blood and brain, and kind of a bloody water." Hargis' instinct was that the shot had come from in front of the President's limousine, since he was riding at the left rear of the car and the blood and brain tissue had been blown back onto him and his motorcycle. Hargis quickly parked his motorcycle and ran up the grassy knoll to the picket fence and the railroad yard. Hargis remembers seeing only one man in the yard, which he assumed was a railroad detective that had just come into the area. Hargis then returned to his motorcycle and started talking to witnesses.

Lee Bowers Jr. was a railroad tower man for the Union Terminal Company. Mr. Bowers' testimony can be found in Volume VI, page 284 of the 26-volume Warren Report. From his 14-foot tower he had a clear view of the area behind the fence that separated the railroad and parking area from the grassy knoll. Mr. Bowers testified that three cars came into the area from around noon until the time of the shooting at 12:30 P.M. The first was a 1959 blue and white Oldsmobile station wagon with out of state plates and a Goldwater sticker. The second was a black Ford with one man in it, holding something to his face such as a telephone or mike and had Texas license plates. The third was a 1961 or 1962 Chevrolet four-door Impala occupied by one white male. It entered just a few minutes before the shooting, it had out of state license plates, a Goldwater sticker, and was covered with red mud up to the windows. This car cruised the area for a few minutes and then slowly drove back toward the Schoolbook Depository. Bowers said "The last time I saw him he was pausing just about in, just about above the assassination site." Bowers also testified that he saw two men standing behind the fence just before the shots were fired; they were standing 10 or 15 feet apart and looking over the fence toward the Presidential motorcade as it approached. Mr. Bowers, in his testimony before the Warren Commission, stated that he heard three shots—the first shot, a pause, then two shots in rapid succession. When asked about a commotion that had caught his eye during the shooting for some reason, Mr. Bowers said, "Nothing that I could pinpoint as having happened that_____". Mr. Bowers was cut off by an unrelated question about a different subject. A short time later Mr. Bowers was excused as a witness without ever explaining what had caught his eye.

Mark Lane taped and filmed an interview with Mr. Bowers in 1966, and in his book, *RUSH TO JUDGEMENT*, Mark Lane writes: "Bowers: At the time of the shooting in the vicinity of where the two men I described were, there was a flash of light or, as far as I am concerned, something I could not identify, but there was something which occurred which caught my eye in this immediate area on the embankment. Now, what this was, I could not state at that time and at this time I could not identify it, other than there was some unusual occurrence.......a flash of light or smoke or something out of the ordinary had occurred there."

S. M. Holland was the Signal Supervisor for the Union Terminal Railroad. He had been employed by the railroad for 25 years and was standing on the triple underpass when the shooting occurred. In his testimony before the Warren Commission, Mr. Holland gave an excellent recollection of what was happening in the Presidential limousine at the time of the first two shots. Mr. Holland thought he had heard three or four shots. I will quote Mr. Holland: "There was a shot, a report, I don't know if it was a shot. I can't say that. And a puff of smoke came out about six or eight feet above the ground right out from under those trees. And at just about this location from where I was standing you could see that puff of smoke, like someone had thrown a firecracker, or something out, and that is just about the way it sounded. It wasn't as loud as the previous reports or shots." Mr. Holland was talking about the trees just behind the picket fence at the top of the grassy knoll. When asked about which shot, he replied, "The third or fourth." Mr. Holland was then asked if he had any doubt about that and he replied, "I have no doubt about seeing that puff of smoke come out from under those trees." Mr. Holland had also made a statement in the Dallas County Sheriff's office immediately after the assassination of President Kennedy on November 22, 1963. In that statement he had said, "I looked over toward the arcade and trees and saw a puff of smoke come from under the trees."

Austin L. Miller worked for the Louisana Freight Bureau and was standing on the triple underpass at the time of the assassination of President Kennedy. After the shooting, Mr. Miller was immediately taken to the Sheriff's office to make a statement about what he had witnessed. In the statement that he made that day, November 22, 1963, Mr. Miller states, "I saw something which I thought was smoke or steam coming from a group of trees north of Elm." Mr. Miller also testified before the Warren Commission, where Assistant Counsel David Belin took his deposition. The smoke or steam coming from the trees that Mr. Miller had witnessed seeing during the shooting was never brought up in Mr. Miller's deposition.

Gordon Arnold was on leave from the Army and wanted to film the President's motorcade. He was in his Army uniform and wanted to film from atop the triple underpass, but a well-dressed man with a badge prevented him from doing so. Mr. Arnold then found a spot at the top of the grassy knoll, a few feet in front of the picket fence, to shoot his movie film. During the shooting, he felt a shot whiz by his left ear and threw himself to the ground. When questioned by a uniformed officer a few moments later, he insisted to the officer that the shots came from behind him. The officer confiscated his movie film, and the next day Gordon Arnold shipped out for a tour of duty in the Army. Mr. Arnold never testified before the Warren Commission. In 1978, Gordon Arnold was interviewed by the DALLAS MORNING NEWS, and at that time there were some who doubted his story. Nevertheless, U.S. Senator Ralph Yarborough who was riding two cars behind the President's car with Vice President Lyndon Johnson soon corroborated it. Senator Yarborough had read the MORNING NEWS article about

Gordon Arnold, and had written the newspaper that he recalled that during the shooting "he saw a uniformed man immediately hit the dirt at the spot where Arnold said he was filming." The Senator remembered thinking to himself at the time that the soldier's quick reaction suggested he must be a real combat veteran. What happened to the confiscated film and whom the officer was that took it are unknown.

In growing up with a rifle in my hand, I had never seen a puff of smoke come out of a rifle barrel when it was fired. In asking around, however, I found that a well-oiled rifle barrel would cause a puff of smoke to come out of the barrel upon firing. Then, when the Gulf War broke out, I was watching a film clip of Saddam Hussein on television and Hussein fired a rifle into the air. A large puff of smoke came from the end of the barrel.

THE SECOND MURDER

After Oswald was confronted in the Schoolbook Depository lunchroom by Officer Baker and identified as an employee of the depository by Roy Truly, he bought a coke from the coke machine in the lunchroom and casually walked out the front door of the depository. Oswald then walked down Elm Street and caught a bus, but the bus was stalled in traffic. Oswald asked the bus driver for a transfer and that transfer was on Oswald when he was arrested. The transfer was stamped at 12:40 P.M. Oswald then walked to near the Greyhound bus station and caught a taxi to the 500 block of North Beckley in the Oak Cliff section of Dallas, about five blocks from where he had rented a room from Earlene Roberts at 1026 North Beckley a month earlier for $8.00 a week. At the time he rented the room, Oswald told Mrs. Roberts his name was O. H. Lee. Oswald was separated from his wife Marina at the time, but did spend weekends with Marina and the children at the Paine residence in Irving. Oswald rushed into Mrs. Robert's house at about one o'clock on November 22, 1963, and went straight to his room. Mrs. Roberts remembers that Oswald was in shirtsleeves when he came in, but when he emerged from his room he had on a jacket. As Oswald rushed out of the house, Mrs. Roberts commented, "My, you're sure in a hurry." Oswald did not answer her.

At 12:54 P.M. Dallas Police Officer J. D. Tippit called in his location as he cruised the Oak Cliff area. Tippit was told to remain at large in that area and was given a rough description of Oswald as it was known at that time. At 1:18 P.M. a citizen came on Tippit's police radio and said "Hello, police operator." The citizen was told to go ahead and the citizen reported the shooting of Officer Tippit and gave the address. An eyewitness to the shooting said that Officer Tippit had stopped a man walking down the street and the man then casually stepped over to the police car and asked "What was up." Officer Tippit opened the door and stepped out of the police car. He and the man stood there for a moment face to face, and then the man pulled out a gun and shot Officer Tippit for no apparent reason, pumping four shots into Tippit at point blank range. Officer Tippit was already dead when the man then ran down the street with the pistol in his hand. Witnesses gave a description of the man and Dallas Police converged on the area, beginning a systematic search. A few minutes later, a theater cashier called police and reported a suspicious "wild looking" man who had just entered the Texas theater on West Jefferson Street. Several squad cars converged on the theater, and several officers entered from the front while Officer N. N. McDonald went in the rear exit door. The movie, "War is Hell," was showing. Officer McDonald walked up the aisle, and as he was questioning a movie patron, he noticed Lee Harvey Oswald sitting three rows away. As Officer McDonald approached, Oswald jumped up and said, "This is it. It's all over now," and slammed his fist into Officer McDonald's face. Oswald reached for his pistol under his shirt and the two men grappled for control of the gun. Oswald had his hand on the trigger with the barrel pointing straight at McDonald. When Oswald squeezed the trigger, however, the gun went click; it was a misfire. Other officers came running, and after a violent struggle, Oswald was disarmed. Officers rushed Oswald into a police car and he was taken to the Dallas city jail.

Three bullets were removed from Officer J. D. Tippit's body, and along with Oswald's .38 special Smith and Wesson revolver, they were sent to the F.B.I. laboratory for testing. Test bullets were fired from the .38 special and compared to the bullets removed from Tippit. In a letter from F.B.I. Director J. Edgar Hoover to Dallas Chief of Police Jesse Curry, the letter read in part "A portion of the surface of each bullet is mutilated, however, microscopic marks remain on these bullets for comparison purposes. The bullets were compared with each other and with test bullets obtained from Oswald's revolver. No conclusion could be reached whether or not the bullets removed from Officer Tippit were fired from the same weapon or whether or not they were fired from Oswald's revolver."

DALLAS POLICE HEADQUARTERS

It was about 2 P.M. on November 22, 1963, and I was sitting in homicide at Dallas Police Headquarters giving a statement to Detective Gus Rose concerning what I had witnessed in Dealey Plaza that day. Mr. Rose was taking notes on his pad. Suddenly there was a commotion and a disheveled young man was brought into the homicide office. The man was handcuffed and when Gus Rose asked one of the officers who the man was, the officer replied, "He is the man who just killed a policeman in Oak Cliff." I was immediately dismissed, but would learn on television that evening that this man was Lee Harvey Oswald.

Soon after Oswald was brought into the homicide office by the arresting officers, a group of investigators started assembling in the office. They included a Secret Service Agent, an F.B.I. Agent, a Texas Ranger, and Captain Will Fritz, the head of the Dallas Homicide Bureau, plus others. Oswald was interrogated for most of the rest of the afternoon. The interrogation of Oswald was a three-ring circus, with officers and agents from all branches of government wanting to be part of the investigation. Captain Fritz felt he should be in charge of the interrogation and should be able to talk to Oswald alone, as was proper and considered good procedure. Due to pressure from the F.B.I. and the Secret Service, neither Fritz nor anyone else ever had a chance to interrogate Oswald in a one-on-one situation. Oswald vehemently denied any involvement in the assassination of President Kennedy or anything else. Those present during the interrogation said Oswald was arrogant, noncommittal, and tight-lipped. Oswald was offered cold drinks, given breaks, and taken to the rest room. He was not pressured, coerced, or harassed, and the interrogators went out of their way not to place Oswald under duress. At about 4 o'clock, Oswald asked if he could make a phone call and it was arranged. Oswald tried to make the call, but could not reach the party he was trying to call. He did complete the call later in the day and talked for about 30 minutes. After about four hours of interrogation, the officers and agents present felt their interrogation was going nowhere. Oswald still denied any knowledge of the assassination of President Kennedy and the murder of Officer Tippit. At about 7:00 P.M. on November 22, 1963, the Dallas Police filed murder charges against Lee Harvey Oswald for the murder of Dallas Police Officer J. D. Tippit. Shortly after the murder charge was filed, Oswald was transferred from the third floor homicide office up to the city jail on the fifth floor. As Oswald came down the hall to the elevator to go up to the jail, reporters took photographs, and when Oswald was asked about the assassination by a reporter, he replied, "I don't know where you people get your information. I haven't committed any acts of violence." When Oswald reached the jail, he was stripped and searched. Any item such as his belt, that might be used to harm himself, was taken from him. He was placed in a maximum security cell and all other prisoners in adjacent cells were moved. A guard was placed outside his cell. Later that evening the President of the Dallas Bar Association, Louis Nichols, was escorted to Oswald's cell to confer with Oswald. Oswald spurned any assistance by the Dallas bar, but Nichols was able to advise Oswald of his legal rights. Oswald indicated to Nichols that he wanted a New York Attorney named John Apt to defend him, and if he was not available, someone with the American Civil Liberties Union.

During the evening, F.B.I. agents repeatedly asked Dallas Chief of Police Jesse Curry to turn over all the evidence on Oswald to them. By midnight, Chief Curry relented, with the condition that once the evidence was tested in the F.B.I. laboratory it would be returned to the Dallas Police Department.

Around midnight, rumors among the throng of reporters who had gathered in Dallas were that Oswald was being badly treated by the Dallas Police. The Dallas Police were well aware of the image they must maintain to the world and a press conference was hastily arranged shortly after midnight to let the press see Oswald's physical condition and take pictures of Oswald. The reporters were told, and they agreed, to only take pictures and observe Oswald's physical condition. Oswald was then brought down to where the press had assembled, and when Oswald entered the room, he was hit by a barrage of questions from the reporters trying to get statements from him. It was pandemonium and Oswald was soon taken back to his jail cell. He was then taken to the Identification section to be fingerprinted and have his photograph taken for police files. It was now 1:10 A.M., November 23, 1963. At about 1:30 A.M., Oswald was taken to the fourth floor and arraigned for the murder of President John F. Kennedy by Justice of the Peace David Johnson. Oswald responded to the arraignment with, "I don't know what you are talking about. What's the idea of this. What are you doing this for?" Oswald was once again returned to his cell. This time he was left alone for the rest of the night.

On Saturday, November 23, 1963, Dallas Police Chief Jesse Curry announced to the world in front of television cameras "Oswald is the man who killed the President." In less than 24 hours Lee Harvey Oswald had been tried, convicted, and found guilty.

In the nearly two days that Oswald was in the Dallas city jail, Oswald was interrogated by local, state, and federal officials. No taped or written records were made of these interrogations; however, in November of 1997 the Assassination Records Review Board did acquire Dallas Homicide Chief, Captain J. W. "Will" Fritz's handwritten notes on Oswald's interrogation. Captain Fritz told the Warren Commission in 1964 that he took no notes during the interrogation, but indicated that he later typed a report based on rough notes that were made several days later. Captain Fritz's notes do reveal Oswald stated "he was in the second floor lunch room of the Schoolbook Depository drinking a coke when the assassination occurred. Local, state, and federal interrogators who were present have all stated that Oswald repeatedly denied any guilt.

At 11:21 A.M. Sunday morning November 24, 1963, Oswald was ushered out into the basement of Dallas Police Headquarters to be transferred to the Dallas County jail. Jack Ruby jumped out of the crowd of mostly reporters and shot and killed Lee Harvey Oswald with one shot in full view of millions of television viewers.

Soon after Oswald's death a press conference was held and Dallas County District Attorney Henry Wade told the world that "there is no question that Oswald was the killer."

It has been reported from reliable sources that the White House sent Dallas Police Chief Jesse Curry a message that fateful weekend stating "it is important to quell any speculation about a conspiracy behind the assassination."

THE NOTES OF THE FINAL INTERROGATION OF LEE HARVEY OSWALD AT DALLAS POLICE HEADQUARTERS

For years, there has been much criticism over the fact that no notes or tape recordings of the interrogation of Lee Harvey Oswald were made at Dallas Police Headquarters. The fact is that there were detailed notes taken during Oswald's final interrogation. A memorandum of these detailed notes are in the 26 volumes of the Warren Report. These notes were not taken by anyone with the Dallas Police, the Secret Service, or the FBI, but by a U.S. Postal inspector. It must be noted that the Assassination

Records Review Board in the 90's did discover some very brief notes made some 30 years earlier by Dallas Police Captain Will Fritz that were taken during these interrogations and these brief notes are now in the National Archives. The brief notes taken by Captain Fritz notes correspond with the much more detailed notes of those taken by Harry D. Holmes, a Dallas Postal Inspector who also witnessed the assassination through binoculars from his fifth floor office in the postal building opposite the Schoolbook Depository in Dealey Plaza. Mr. Holmes was also present and participated in Oswald's last interrogation at Dallas Police Headquarters on Sunday morning November 24, 1963, just before Jack Ruby killed Oswald in the basement of Dallas Police Headquarters. Mr. Holmes' memorandum of this interrogation can be found in volume XXIV, pages 488 to 492 and is labeled Commission Exhibit No. 2064. This Commission exhibit, 2064, reads as follows:

> On December 17, 1963, Mr. Harry Holmes, Postal Inspector U.S. Post Office, Terminal Annex, Dallas Texas, made available to Special Agent Charles T. Brown Jr. a copy of a memorandum reflecting results of interview by Inspector Holmes with Lee Harvey Oswald on November 24, 1963, which memorandum is quoted as follows.
>
> "Dallas, Texas December 17, 1963
> MEMORANDOM OF INTERVIEW"
>
> Informal memorandum furnished by Postal Inspector H. D. Holmes, Dallas, Texas, of an interview he took part in with Lee H. Oswald on Sunday morning, November 24, 1963, between the approximate hours of 9:25 a.m. to 11:10 a.m. Those present, in addition to Inspector Holmes, were Captain Will Fritz, Dallas Police, Forrest V. Sorrels, Local Agent in Charge, Secret Service, and Thomas J. Kelly, Inspector, Secret Service. In addition, there were three Detectives who where apparently assigned to guarding Oswald as none of them took part in the interrogation.
>
> "Oswald at no time appeared confused or in doubt as to whether or not he should answer a question. On the contrary, he was quite alert and showed no hesitancy in answering those questions which he wanted to answer, and quite skillful in parrying those questions which he did not want to answer. I got the impression that he had disciplined his mind and reflexes to a state where I personally doubted if he would ever have confessed. He denied emphatically having taken part in or having any knowledge of the shooting of the Policeman Tippitt, or the President, stating that so far as he is concerned the reason he was in custody was because he 'popped a policeman in the nose in a theater on Jefferson Avenue.'
>
> "P.O. BOXES—He was questioned separately about the three boxes he had rented, and in each instance his answers were quick, direct and accurate as reflected on the box rental applications. He stated without prompting that he had rented Box 2915 at the Main Post Office for several months prior to his going to New Orleans, that this box was rented in his own name, Lee H. Oswald, and that he had taken out two keys to the box, and that when he closed the box, he directed that his mail be forwarded to his street address in New Orleans.
>
> "He stated that no one received mail in this box other than himself, nor did he receive any mail under any other name than his own true name; that no one had access to the box other than himself nor did he permit anyone else to use this box. He stated it was possible that on rare occasions he may have handed one of the keys to his wife to go get his mail but certainly nobody else. He denied emphatically that he ever ordered a rifle under his name on any other name, nor permitted anyone else to order a rifle to be received in this box. Further, he denied that he had ever ordered any rifle by mail order or bought any money order for the purpose of paying for such a rifle. In fact, he claimed he owned no rifle and had not practiced or shot a rifle other than possibly a .22 small bore rifle, since his days in the Marine Corp. He stated 'How could I afford to order a

rifle on my salary of $1.25 an hour when I can't hardly feed myself on what I make.'

"When asked if he had a post office box in New Orleans he stated that he did, for the reason that he subscribed to several publications, at least two of which were published in Russia, one being the hometown paper published in Minsk where he had met and married his wife, and that he moved around so much that it was more practical to simply rent post office boxes and have his mail forwarded from one box to the next rather than going through the process of furnishing changes of address to the publishers. When asked if he permitted anyone other than himself to get mail in box 30051 in New Orleans, he stated that he did not. It will be recalled that on this box rent application he showed that both Marina Oswald and A.J. Hidell were listed under the caption 'persons entitled to receive mail through box.' After denying that anyone else was permitted to get mail in the box, he was reminded that this application showed the name Marina Oswald as being entitled to receive mail in the box and he replied 'well so what, she was my wife and I see nothing wrong with that, and it could very well be that I did place her name on the application.' He was then reminded that the application also showed the name A.J. Hidell was also entitled to receive mail in the box, at which he simply shrugged his shoulders and stated 'I don't recall anything about that.'

"He stated that when he came back to Dallas and after he had gone to work for the Texas School Book Depository, he had rented a box at the nearby Terminal Annex postal station, this being box 6225, and that this box was also rented in his name, Lee H. Oswald. He stated he had only checked out one key for this box, which information was found to be accurate, and this key was found on his person at the time of his arrest. He professed not to recall the fact that he showed on the box rental application under name of corporation 'Fair Play For Cuba Committee' and 'American Civil Liberties Union.' When asked as to why he showed these organizations on his application, he simply shrugged and said that he didn't recall showing them. When asked if he paid the box rental or did the organizations pay it, he stated that he paid it. In answer to another question, he also stated that no one had any knowledge that he had this box other than himself.

ORGANIZATIONS-MEMBERSHIP IN — With respect to American Civil Liberties Union he was a little evasive stating something to the effect that he had made some effort to join but it was never made clear whether he had or had not been accepted. He stated that he first became interested in the Fair Play For Cuba Committee, after he went to New Orleans, that it started out as being a group of individuals who, like him, who thought and had like political opinions. They did decide to organize, and did organize after a fashion, but denied that they had any president or elected officers. He stated that he, himself, could probably be considered the secretary since he wrote some letters on their behalf and attempted to collect dues, which, if I recall, where $1.00 per month. He also stated that there was a 'Fair Play For Cuba Committee' in New York which was better organized. He denied that he was sent to Dallas for the purpose of organizing such a cell in Dallas.

"When asked if he was a communist, he stated emphatically not, that he was a Marxist. Someone asked the difference and he stated that a communist is a Lenin-Marxist, that he himself was a pure Marxist, and when someone asked the difference, he stated that it was a long story and if they didn't know, it would take too long to tell them. He stated further that he had read about everything written by or about Karl Marx.

"When asked as to his religion, he stated that Karl Marx was his religion, and in his response to further questioning he stated that some people may find the bible interesting reading, but it was not for him, stating further that even as a philosophy there was not much to the bible.

MARINE CORP_SERVICE—Captain Fritz made some mention of his dishonorable discharge from the Marine Corp at which point he bristled noticeably, stating that he had been discharged with an 'honorable' discharge and that this was later changed due to his having attempted to denounce his American Citizenship while he was living in Russia. He stated further that since his change of citizenship did not come to pass, he had written a letter to Mr. Connally, then Secretary of the Navy, and after considerable delay, received a very respectful reply wherein Connally stated he had resigned to run for governor of Texas, and that his letter was being referred to the new secretary, a Mr.

Cork, Kurth, or something like that. He showed no particular animosity toward Mr. Connally while discussing this feature.

MAP—Captain Fritz advised him that among his effects in his room, there was found a map of the city of Dallas that had some marks on it and asked him to explain this map. Oswald said he presumed he had reference to an old City map on which he had made some X's denoting location of firms that had advertised job vacancies. He stated that he had no transportation and either walked or rode a bus and that as he was constantly looking for work, in fact had registered at the Texas Employment Bureau, and that as he would receive leads either from newspaper ads or from the bureau or from neighbors, he would chart these places on the map to save time in his traveling. He said to the best of his recollection, most of them were out Industrial, presumably meaning Industrial Blvd. When asked why the X at the location of the Texas School Book Depository at Elm and Houston, he stated that 'Well, I interviewed there for a job, in fact, got the job, therefore the X.

"When asked as to how he learned about this vacancy, he stated that 'Oh, it was general information in the neighborhood, I don't recall just who told me about it, but I learned it from people in Mrs. Paynes neighborhood and that all the people around there were looking out for possible employment for him."

ACTIVITY JUST PRIOR TO AND IMMEDIATELY FOLLOWING ASSASSINATION ATTEMPT—To an inquiry as to why he went to visit his wife on Thursday night, November 21, whereas he normally visited her over the weekend, he stated that on this particular weekend he had learned that his wife and Mrs. Payne were giving a party for the children and that they were having in a 'houseful' of neighborhood children and that he just didn't want to be around at such time. Therefore, he made his weekly visit on Thursday night.

"When asked if he didn't bring a sack with him the next morning to work, he stated that he did, and when asked as to the contents of the sack, he stated that it contained his lunch. Then when asked to the size or shape of the sack, he said 'Oh, I don't recall, it may have been a small sack or a large sack, you don't always find one that just fits your sandwiches. When asked as to where he placed the sack when he got into the car, he said in his lap, or possibly the front seat beside him, as he always did because he didn't want to get it crushed. He denied that he placed any package in the back seat. When advised that the driver stated that he had brought out a long parcel and placed it in the back seat, he stated 'Oh, he must be mistaken or else thinking about some other time when he picked me up.'

"When asked about his whereabouts at the time of the shooting, he stated that when lunch time came, and he didn't say which floor he was on, he said one of the negro employees invited him to eat lunch with him and he stated 'You go on down and send the elevator back up and I will join you in a few minutes.' Before he could finish whatever he was doing, he stated, the commotion surrounding the assassination took place and when he went down stairs, a policeman questioned him as to his identification and his boss stated that 'he is one of our employees' whereupon the policeman had him step aside momentarily. Following this, he simply walked out the front door of the building. I don't recall that anyone asked why he left or where or how he went. I just presumed that this had been covered in an earlier questioning.

A.J. HIDELL IDENTIFICATION CARD—Captain Fritz asked him if he knew anyone by the name of A. J. Hidell and he denied that he did. When asked if he had ever used this name as an alias, he also made a denial. In fact, he stated that he had never had heard of the name before. Captain Fritz then asked him about the I.D. card he had in his pocket bearing such a name and he flared up and stated 'I've told you all I'm going to about that card. You took notes, just read them for yourself, if you want to refresh your memory.' He told Captain Fritz that 'You have the card, now you know as much about it as I do.'

"About 11:00 a.m. or a few minutes thereafter, someone handed through the door several hangers on which there were some trousers, shirts, and a couple of sweaters. When asked if he wanted to change any of his clothes before being transferred to the County jail, he said, 'just give me one of those sweaters.'

"He didn't like the one they handed him and insisted on putting on a black slip-over sweater that had some jagged holes in it near the front of the right shoulder. One cuff was released while he slipped this over his head, following which he was again cuffed. During this change of clothing, Chief of Police Curry came into the room and discussed something in an inaudible undertone with Captain Fritz, apparently for the purpose of not letting Oswald hear what was being said. I have no idea what this conversation was, but just presume they were discussing the transfer of the prisoner. I did not go downstairs to witness the further transfer of the prisoner."

s/ H. D. Holmes

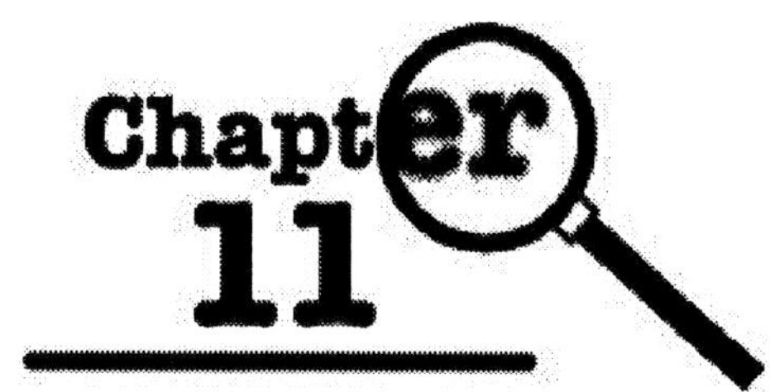

THE AUTOPSY

The autopsy of President John F. Kennedy is at the center of the controversy of what really happened in Dealey Plaza at 12:30 P.M. on November 22, 1963. The official autopsy results did not agree with what the nurses and doctors at Parkland Hospital had observed concerning President Kennedy's head injuries when the President was brought into the emergency room and attended to at Parkland. Through the nearly forty years since the assassination, the more the researchers and medical experts have delved into the official autopsy results, the more problems they find with it. First of all, the doctor put in charge of the autopsy, Naval Commander Dr. James J. Humes, had no real qualification for doing the autopsy except his high rank in the Navy. Dr. Humes had completed a course in forensic pathology in medical school, but had never practiced forensic pathology. Dr Humes' position with the Navy was Director of Laboratories at the Bethesda Naval Hospital, and he had never performed an autopsy involving gunshot wounds. I do not want to take anything away from Dr. Humes. By all accounts he was a fine man, a competent man, but autopsies were not an every day thing for Dr. Humes. Secondly, there was no attempt by the Warren Commission to reconcile the differences in what the doctors and nurses at Parkland had observed and what was on the autopsy report. In fact, the observations of doctors, nurses, and other witnesses, that the back of the President's head had been blown out, was ignored by the Warren Commission in its final conclusion.

In closely studying the documents and other facts concerning the autopsy, there is evidence that the <u>preliminary</u> autopsy findings did agree with the doctors, nurses, and other witnesses, that the right rear of the President's head had been blown away. That doctor Humes destroyed his initial autopsy report and did not make a final autopsy report until December 6, 1963, is at the top of the list. Later chapters will help you understand why I make this statement. We do know, that for some undisclosed reason, the military personnel present were ordered to never discuss what they had witnessed during the autopsy of the President under threat of court martial.

The President's body was flown back to Washington D.C. on Air Force One shortly after being pronounced dead on November 22, 1963. Upon arrival in Washington, his corpse was taken to Bethesda Naval Hospital for an autopsy. The autopsy started at about 8 P.M. EST, November 22, 1963. Naval Commander James J. Humes of the Medical Corps, United States Navy, was in charge of the autopsy. Naval Commander Dr. J. Thornton Boswell and Marine Lt. Col. Pierre A. Finck were Dr. Humes' main assistants. There were x-ray technicians, various medical technicians, photographers, F.B.I. agents, Secret Service agents, and other military personnel present. There were no civilians present. What should have been one of the most thorough and complete autopsies ever performed was not close to being thorough and/or complete, even by military standards, when one views the "official" autopsy report.

The autopsy report about the head injury moved the gaping hole in the back of the President's head up somewhat. It does acknowledge that part of the back of the head is missing and I will quote: "There is a large irregular defect of the scalp and skull on the right involving chiefly the parietal bone but extending somewhat into the temporal and occipital regions. In this region there is an actual absence of scalp and bone producing a defect which measures approximately 13cm in greatest diameter." In layman's terms, it reads: "There is a large hole in the scalp and skull on the right involving chiefly the top of the head but extending into the side and back of the head. The scalp and skull are actually missing and the hole measures five and one quarter inches across." What has confused many experts and medical personnel who have studied the autopsy report is that the undeveloped photo negatives and x-rays taken during the autopsy were turned over to the F.B.I. and replaced with drawings made two days later by an artist who had never seen the President's head or the undeveloped photos! (See pages 65 and 66.) These drawings do not depict what the doctors, nurses, and other witnesses observed. To further complicate the matter, the Warren Commission only used the artist drawings to come to their final conclusions. Dr. Humes, in his testimony before the Warren Commission, admitted the drawings were not to scale.

What was left of the President's brain was a vital piece of evidence. The brain was removed during the autopsy and was put into a formalin solution so that it could be sectioned to trace the path of the bullet or bullets through the brain. It is acknowledged in the autopsy report that there were some small brain specimens removed from the brain for analyses, but regarding sectioning the brain to trace the path of a bullet or bullets, there is the notation, "In the interest of preserving the specimen, coronal sections are not made." The preserved brain of the President then disappeared and has never been found. This raises serious questions. Did someone actually lose the brain of the President of the United States without a trace, or was it dissected as scheduled in accordance with correct autopsy procedure and the dissection of the brain revealed that the fatal headshot had in fact hit the President from the front, which would confirm a conspiracy? Or did the dissection of the brain reveal that the President's head had been hit by two bullets, which would also confirm a conspiracy? Was the brain destroyed deliberately upon learning from the dissection that it pointed to a conspiracy? Will we ever know the truth about the fate of this most vital piece of evidence?

Dr. Humes, in his testimony before the Warren Commission admitted that he had purposely burned his original autopsy notes and then rewrote the "official" notes two days later. His excuse was "the original notes, which were stained with the blood of our late President, I felt were inappropriate to retain" and that the President's personal physician, Dr. Burkley, had authorized Dr. Humes to destroy the original notes.

We also know that the military autopsy findings about the throat wound were at odds with what the attending physicians and nurses at Dallas Parkland Hospital had observed. When the President was rushed into the emergency room at Parkland, one of the first things noticed was a small round entrance wound to the throat. This throat entrance wound was promptly widened with a scalpel to do a tracheotomy on the President. When Dr. Humes performed the autopsy on the President later that evening, the throat wound went unnoticed. It was not until the next morning, when Dr. Humes called Dr. Perry, one of the attending physicians at Parkland, that Dr. Humes learned of the throat wound. Yet this unobserved throat wound during the autopsy was deemed an exit wound in the autopsy report by Dr. Humes. That Dr. Humes declared the throat wound an exit wound, a wound he admittedly had not observed, and despite what Dr. Perry had told him, raises more questions about the accuracy of the autopsy report. When Dr. Malcolm Perry was interviewed again in 1979, he was still adamant that the throat wound was an entrance wound. An entry wound is small and an exit wound is large. For example, when emergency room nurse Margaret Henchliffe, who had witnessed numerous gunshot wounds in Parkland's emergency room, testified before the Warren Commission, she was asked by Assistant Council Arlen Spector if the throat wound was an exit wound and she replied without hesitation "I have never seen an exit hole look like that."

The President's back wound was crucial in determining if one bullet had penetrated both the President and the Governor. The official autopsy report diagram showed that the bullet that had hit the President in the back was about six inches below the collar in the shoulder and not the neck. The President's shirt and coat had bullet holes in them about six inches below the collar and none in the neck. The death certificate signed by the President's personal physician, Dr. George Burkley, states that the non-fatal back wound was, "In the back at about the level of the third thoracic vertebra." The artist drawing placed the back injury in the President's neck at collar level. The Warren Commission used the artist drawing (page 65, exhibit 385) to determine the path of the bullet in determining that one bullet penetrated both men. The bullet that hit the President in the back was reportedly fired from six stories up. Since the back wound was about six inches below the collar that puts the back wound below the front neck wound. A downward moving bullet does not alter its trajectory in soft flesh and suddenly start going up. That the back wound was six inches below the collar and below the front neck wound makes it impossible for that shot to have hit both the President and Governor Connally. The back wound could only be probed about an inch, which raised more questions. Was the back wound the result of a dud, and that is why the first shot sounded like a firecracker or an engine backfire? Was the pristine bullet found on the floor at Parkland the bullet that had worked its way out of the President's back?

There was a large piece of the President's skull found in Dealey Plaza shortly after the shooting; it was lying near the curb where the fatal headshot had occurred. It was a piece of occipital bone, the bone at the back of the skull. The artist drawing that the Warren Commission used did not show any of the occipital bone missing; instead it shows the back of the head intact. This one piece of bone from the rear of the President's head was hard factual physical evidence that the back of the President's skull had been blown out from a frontal shot. This piece of skull was preserved in the National Archives after the Warren Commission made its final report. It has now disappeared from the National Archives and cannot be found. Fortunately, it was photographed and the photograph is still available.

We know that small minute bullet fragments were removed from President Kennedy's head during the autopsy. We also know that a "missile," not a fragment, was removed from the President's body during the autopsy and was also signed for by F.B.I. agents James Sibert and Frank O'Neil, and that this bullet never again surfaced in the investigation. That this missile was a whole bullet was confirmed by Admiral Calvin Galloway, who was present at the autopsy.

We also know that when White House Assistant Press Secretary Malcolm Kilduff announced to the press and the world at Parkland Hospital shortly after 1 P.M. on November 22, 1963 that the

President was dead, he pointed to his right temple as the point of entrance of the fatal shot that killed the President.

We learned in 1976, when the House on Assassination's Committee was formed to re-investigate the assassination of President Kennedy, that many of the items listed in the official inventory of the autopsy materials were missing. We also learned that Floyd Riebe, a medical photographic technician who took the autopsy pictures at the autopsy, said that the President's head had a gaping hole in the back. When Riebe was shown two pictures from the autopsy, he replied, "The two pictures you showed me are not what I saw that night, it's being phonied someplace" We found out that Jerrol Custer, the x-ray technician who took x-rays at the autopsy, was shown a supposedly official autopsy x-ray, and was asked "Is this an x-ray you took?" Mr. Custer replied by placing his hand at the back of his head and said, "No, this area was gone, there was no scalp there." It is also a fact that the x-rays and photographs shown in 1976 do not relate to each other. Dr. Robert McClellen, one of the attending physicians at Parkland Hospital, also denied the authenticity of these so-called official autopsy x-rays.

The Warren Commission members did have a lively debate about many of the above issues, and did closely study the admittedly hastily made drawings, but still, in the end, determined that all of President Kennedy's wounds resulted from gunshots from the rear and not the front. Dr. Humes, in his testimony to the Warren Commission concerning the autopsy on the President, spoke in medical terminology and not one member of the Warren Commission had any medical training.

COMMISSION EXHIBIT 385

Erroneous depiction of bullet entrance.

COMMISSION EXHIBIT 386

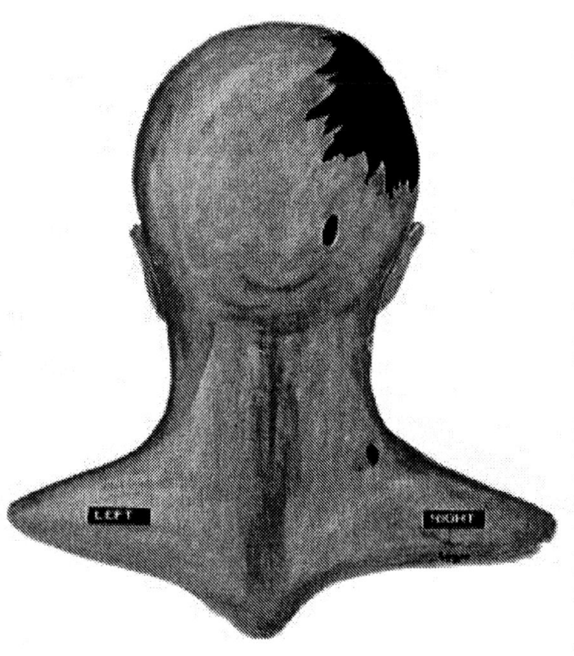

Back wound was actually 6" lower than artist's depiction.

COMMISSION EXHIBIT 388

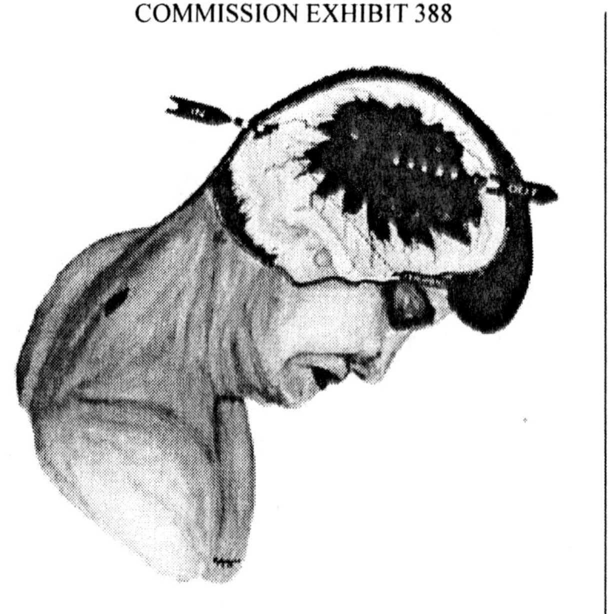

This illustration does not correspond to autopsy witness and photo descriptions.

WASHINGTON D.C., NOVEMBER 24, 1963

SATISFY THE PUBLIC

Today, the word "spin" in political circles is common. To "spin" something, as we know it today, is to put your views on a subject into a certain verbal image that influences what you want others to think and believe about that subject, regardless of what the actual truth is. In 1963, most of us had never heard of "spin." But "spin" was already alive and well in Washington D.C. on November 24, 1963, two days after the assassination of John F. Kennedy. When Jack Ruby killed Lee Harvey Oswald in front of millions of viewers on television that Sunday morning, a closed-door secret meeting was hastily assembled by top government officials. We do not know all of whom were in attendance at this meeting, but we do know of at least two men who were there, because one wrote a memorandum that surfaced years later. That man was Nicolas Katzenbach, Deputy United States Attorney General under Attorney General Robert Kennedy. The other was F.B.I. Director J. Edgar Hoover, who as a result of this meeting, ordered a secret internal F.B.I. memo written to his Bureau chiefs, that also surfaced years later. This meeting was called to discuss how information to the public would be handled concerning the assassination of President Kennedy. <u>What was decided in this meeting would mold in concrete the outcome of any investigation.</u>

It had only been 48 hours since the assassination of President Kennedy when this meeting was held, and there had barely been a preliminary investigation into Lee Harvey Oswald. No other leads had been followed, no commission had been named to investigate, and for all practical purposes, there had been no investigation. The results of this meeting would be the key to why the American public would never know the truth about the assassination of President John F. Kennedy.

On November 24, 1963, shortly after this meeting, Director of the F.B.I., J. Edgar Hoover had an assistant, Agent Jenkins, send a secret memo to F.B.I. Bureau heads. This memo read: "Hoover says Oswald alone did it, bureau must convince the public Oswald is the real assassin."

The next day, November 25, 1963, Nicolas Katzenbach wrote a memorandum to Bill Moyers, who was to be the principal assistant to our new President, Lyndon B. Johnson. The points made in this memorandum were: "It is important that all the facts surrounding President Kennedy's assassination be made public in a way which will satisfy people in the United States and abroad......The public must be satisfied that Oswald was the assassin......that Oswald did not have any confederates who are still at large......that the evidence was such that Oswald would have been convicted at trial......speculation about Oswald's motivation ought to be cut off ......we should have a basis for rebutting thought that this was a conspiracy...... the matter has been handled thus far with neither dignity nor conviction......these objectives may be satisfied by making public a complete and thorough F.B.I. report......there may be inconsistencies between this report and statements by Dallas Police officials......but the reputation of the Bureau is such that it may do the whole job......we need something to head off public speculation or Congressional hearings of the wrong sort......The only other step would be the appointment of a Presidential Commission of unimpeachable personnel to review and examine the evidence and announce its conclusions."

There it was, two of the most powerful and honored men in the United States Justice Department had decided how the results of any investigation would be before there was an investigation. There was to be a cover-up before anyone knew what they were to cover up. Their concern that day, two days after the assassination, was not to find the truth, the facts, of the killing of our President but only to use the prestige of the F.B.I. to convince the public that Oswald was "the real assassin." The next day, November, 26, 1963, only four days after the assassination, Hoover issued another secret internal F.B.I. memo (62-109060-1490) to F.B.I. bureau Chiefs saying, "Wrap up investigation; seems to me we have the basic facts now." F.B.I. Director J. Edgar Hoover also followed up the Katzenbach memorandum to a tee in his report to President Johnson on the assassination of President Kennedy, stating Oswald was a "lone nut assassin," the killer of both police officer Tippit and President Kennedy. He also reiterated that three shots were fired from the Schoolbook Depository—the first shot hit Kennedy in the back, the second shot hit Governor Connally, the third shot hit Kennedy in the head, and there was no conspiracy. Little did the soon to be named seven members of the Warren Commission know that their job was expected to be a rubber stamp for what evidence Hoover and the F.B.I. would feed them. We now know, however, that in one of the Commission's early meetings in January 1964, the newly appointed seven Commission members, to their credit, discussed that they were expected to be Hoover's rubber stamp. One of the Warren Commission members said, "If this is the way it is going to be, we might as well fold up and go home." I cover this early Commission session discussion in another chapter.

THE AFTERMATH

When I left the police station after giving my statement, I headed back to work to find that almost everyone had gone home and the manager was closing the business. I went home, turned on the television, wrote down the events of the day and finally went to bed well after midnight. Saturday morning, November 23, 1963, I went to work only to find a sign on the door that we were closed for the day. I drove around the local neighborhood for a short while, the streets were deserted and I did not see one business open. It was as if Dallas had died too. I went back home and spent the day reading the papers and watching television. The only thing on television, and on every station, was about the assassination of President Kennedy and the wounding of Governor Connally. On television, they ran the same stories over and over again and it did not get old. I watched in amazement, trying to digest the events of yesterday. The newspapers were the same, article after article about the assassination. I read through both newspapers twice, just knowing there would be an article about the missed shot that hit the curb near me during the shooting, but there was nothing.

When I awoke on Sunday morning, November 24,1963, my television was still on and it was one story after another about the assassination on all channels. I got my paper and read every article, and there on page 8, section 1 of THE DALLAS MORNING NEWS was a small article with a small picture of the exact bullet mark that I had seen Friday after the shooting. The heading of the article read "CONCRETE SCAR" and the short article read: "A detective points to a chip in the curb on Houston Street opposite the Schoolbook Depository. A bullet from the rifle that took President Kennedy's life apparently caused the hole." The picture was an actual photograph of the scar on the curb on Main

Street, which Deputy Sheriff Buddy Walthers and I had located moments after the shots had been fired. For some unknown reason the article had placed the location of the curb on Houston Street, not Main Street. That Sunday morning around 11 A.M., I decided to go downtown to a newsstand on Main street and buy a couple of out of town newspapers to see what the rest of the country was saying about the assassination. I had my car radio on as I was driving downtown, and I heard the announcer exclaim "He has been shot, somebody just jumped out of the crowd and shot Lee Harvey Oswald!"

Monday, November 25, 1963, was to be President John F. Kennedy's funeral. I was watching television when a friend knocked on the door. He was a local car dealer that I had spent many an hour with after work, drinking beer and swapping old stories. He asked me if I had anything to drink in the house, and I told him that I did not. He asked me to go with him to get some beer and I did. We drove all over Dallas in search of a beer store, and there was not a business in Dallas that was open that we could find.

On Tuesday, November, 26, 1963, Dallas and the nation went back to work. The only topic of conversation in the workplace was the assassination of President Kennedy and the killing of Oswald by Jack Ruby. I told my friends and co-workers about being in Dealey Plaza, the bullet hitting the curb near me, debris hitting me in the face, and being in the Dallas Police homicide office when they brought Lee Harvey Oswald in. Most were attentive to what I had witnessed, but one or two said that they had not heard anything in the news about a missed shot. The days ran on into December, and the front pages of the newspapers always had a new article about the assassination. Television news did the same, but nothing was said about a missed shot. Then on Friday December 13, 1963 in section 1, page 22 of THE DALLAS MORNING NEWS, the heading read, "QUESTIONS RAISED ON MURDER BULLETS." The article went on to say: "Did a bullet from Lee Harvey Oswald's rifle chip the curb of Main Street near the triple underpass? That question remained unanswered Thursday. And it raised other questions: If one of the three shots from Oswald's mail order rifle struck the curb, is it possible that another bullet ranged through President Kennedy's body and then hit Gov. Connally? If the chip did not result from a bullet, how did it get there? Buddy Walthers, an investigator for Sheriff Bill Decker, found the chipped spot less than an hour after a sniper shot President Kennedy and the governor as their car moved slowly over Elm Street toward the triple underpass. 'A man came up to me and asked if I was hunting for bullets fired at President Kennedy,' Walthers related. 'He said he had stopped his car on Main Street and was standing beside it watching the motorcade, when the shooting started. He said something hit him on the cheek hard enough to sting. I checked the area where the man said he had been standing and found the chip in the curb. It was on the south side of the street.' Main runs parallel to Elm on the south. Walthers and Investigator Allan Sweatt searched the area for about 20 minutes without finding a bullet. They concluded that if a bullet had struck the curb, the slug had ricocheted or disintegrated. The motorist could have been hit by a sliver from the bullet or a particle of concrete from the curb they concluded. The chip appeared freshly made. It was in line with the path a bullet would have taken if fired from the sixth floor of the Schoolbook Depository Building toward the Kennedy motorcade. The trajectory, however, would have carried it above the heads of President Kennedy and the governor. Walthers and Sweatt were within a block of the slaying site when the sniper opened fire. They agreed with other witnesses that the assassin fired only three shots. Gov. Connally said that the first shot struck President Kennedy and the second shot entered his body. Then, the governor related, another bullet struck President Kennedy. That would account for the three shots. It would not, however, account for the chipped spot. Various theories have been advanced. Was Gov. Connally mistaken about what happened during the 10 second period in which the sniper shot him and the President? Did the rifleman fire two bullets into the car, with one striking both President Kennedy and Gov. Connally, and then hurriedly fire a third which passed over their auto? Or did the chipped spot have no connection with the shooting? Couldn't the motorist have been struck by a speck of gravel thrown up by a car? Couldn't the chip have been caused by other gravel? F.B.I. and Secret Service agents may have the answer. But they haven't revealed what they learned during their intensive investigation of the murder of President Kennedy."

I read this article with great interest. As my friends and co-workers had started to wonder if I had been making up the missed shot that hit the curb during the shooting, I felt vindicated by the article. At last, it was coming out now, three weeks later, about a missed shot. The article was generally factual, but not entirely accurate. After reading the article, I had a nagging question in my mind: Should I call the F.B.I. so they could get the facts straight, or should I stay out of it? Deputy Sheriff Walthers had run up to me and asked what happened, not me to him. Once we located the scar on the curb, we had both agreed it was a fresh bullet mark. And what was this about a piece of gravel doing to the curb what a bullet had done? I wrestled with the question of calling the F.B.I. for the rest of the day. Should I call them or not, I kept asking myself. The next morning I woke up thinking that maybe I should go ahead and call the F.B.I. I went to work determined to call them, even starting to place the call three or four times, but I backed out each time. Would the F.B.I. even want to talk to someone like me? They only talk to people with authority, I reasoned, and I am just a country boy, new to the big city and just a new car salesman. Still, the newspaper article was wrong since the bullet had hit the curb on Main Street, not on Houston Street, and the Deputy Sheriff had come running up to me asking what happened, not me running up to him. Besides, it was impossible for gravel to do the damage to the curb that the bullet had done. The newspaper article was just not an accurate account of what really happened concerning the scar on the curb. With knots in my stomach, I finally did pick up the phone and called the F.B.I. Two agents were in my office within an hour.

On December 14, 1963, I was interviewed by two F.B.I. agents at my workplace. They were courteous, but did not seem very interested in what I had to say about a missed shot hitting the curb near where I was standing during the shooting. As they were about to leave, one of the agents asked me if I knew Jack Ruby. I told them that I had met Jack Ruby on a couple of occasions and about being at a local dance hall one evening where Jack Ruby was going from table to table introducing himself and passing out free passes to his strip club. In addition, I told them that my roommate had dated one of his employees. When they left, I had the impression that they already knew about the shot that hit the curb and what I had to say was old news to them.

During the rest of December and into January, the assassination was always in the news. Still there was nothing about a missed shot hitting the curb near where I was standing. If there was an article about the sequence of shots, it was that the first bullet hit the President in the back, the second shot hit Governor Connally in the back, and the third shot hit the President in the head. The news consistently stated that Lee Harvey Oswald was the lone assassin and had fired the shots from the sixth floor of the Texas Schoolbook Depository. It was agreed there was no conspiracy. On November 29, 1963, President Johnson announced the appointment of a Commission to investigate the assassination of President Kennedy. Supreme Court Chief Justice Earl Warren was named to head the seven-man Commission and it was called "The Presidents Commission on the Assassination of President Kennedy." Today it is more commonly known as the Warren Commission.

FD-302 (Rev. 3-3-59) FEDERAL BUREAU OF INVESTIGATION

1

Other Individuals and Organizations Involved or Date 12/16/63

Mr. JIM TAGUE, 2424 Inwood, Apartment 253, employed as a salesman, Chuck Hutton Company, 5431 Lemmon Avenue, Dallas, Texas, advised that he was driving a car on November 22, 1963, and was stopped in traffic at the Triple Underpass located below the Texas School Book Depository (TSBD) Building. While stopped, he saw that the Presidential Motorcade was going to pass nearby, and he got out of his car and stood near the Triple Underpass between Commerce and Main Streets. He stood near the curb of Main Street waiting for the motorcade to come to where he was standing. When the motorcade was approximately 100 feet from him he heard a loud noise, and at that time he looked around as he thought someone had shot a firecracker. He then heard two more loud noises in quick succession. Other persons in the area then started scrambling around, and he realized that the noises must have been gun shots, so he got behind one of the pillars of the underpass. During the time of the shooting, he felt something hit him on his right cheek. Whatever it was that hit him broke the skin and caused about two drops of blood to flow. He thought possibly that one of the bullets had hit the curb near his feet and possibly a piece of the curbing had hit him in the cheek. He did look around the curb and near where he was standing there was a chip missing, which he stated looked fresh. He stated he did not see anyone with a rifle and did not look at the TSBD Building. He did not see the shots take effect and stated he could not furnish any information as to where the shots actually came from. He stated he is not acquainted with OSWALD and had never heard of him prior to the shooting of President KENNEDY.

He has been in JACK RUBY's club on a few occasions, but he actually knows nothing about RUBY, his associations, or his background. He does know RUBY, however, by sight, since he has seen him in his club on a few occasions. TAGUE stated he did not know of any connection or associations between OSWALD and RUBY.

---

on 12/14/63 at Dallas, Texas File # DL 100-10461

by Special Agent HENRY J. OLIVER AND LOUIS M. KELLEY: mam Date dictated 12/16/63

This document contains neither recommendations nor conclusions of the FBI. It is the property of the FBI and is loaned to your agency; it and its contents are not to be distributed outside your agency.

CR 205 5-1

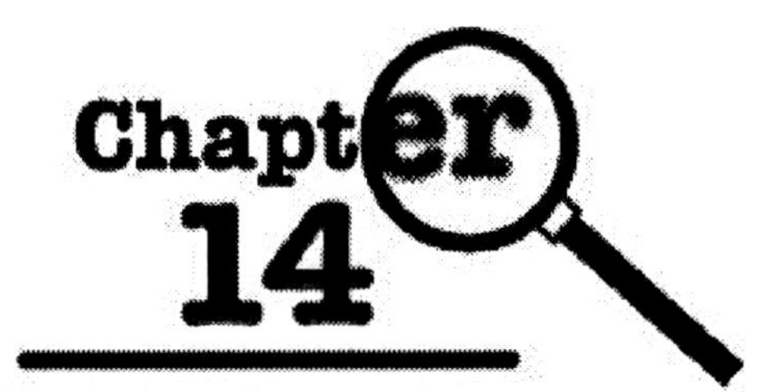

J. EDGAR HOOVER AND THE WARREN COMMISSION

The Warren Commission held one of its first formal meetings in late January 1964 behind closed doors. At that time the public was unaware of the Commission's concerns about what cooperation they would get from J. Edgar Hoover and the F.B.I. Hoover was adamant that Oswald was a lone nut assassin, that three shots had been fired from the sixth floor of the Schoolbook Depository, with the first shot hitting President Kennedy, the second hitting Governor Connally, and the third hitting the President in the head, and that there was no conspiracy.

In the past forty years since the assassination of President Kennedy, we have learned many new facts about the Warren Commission's investigation of the President's assassination. Also, in the last 40 years, we have learned many new facts about J. Edgar Hoover. When you put all of these new facts together, it becomes apparent why there is and has been such a controversy over the Warren Commission findings. We now know that a fair and factual investigation was doomed from the start, caused largely by one man, F.B.I. Director J. Edgar Hoover. Many great and honorable men and women have served in the F.B.I. before and after the assassination of JFK, and I do not want to tarnish the reputations of these honorable agents. One also cannot deny that Hoover did a commendable job in organizing the Bureau into one of the finest law enforcement agencies in the world. Washington writer Jack Anderson once wrote, "Hoover created one of the world's most effective and formidable law enforcement organizations." I know as a young man growing up he was one of my heroes, a man I admired and respected. We now know, however, with what has been made public since his death, that by 1963 he had become bigger and more powerful than any man in this country, in his own mind. His self-centered ego had become so big that he referred to "his" F.B.I. as the "seat of government." He knew politics and how to control politicians better than most Congressmen and Presidents, and he knew how to keep Congressmen and Presidents in line. He kept tabs on up and coming politicians, using his field agents to gather information on their sex habits, morals, ethics, associates, and anything derogatory about them. When he died in 1972, at the age of 77, J. Edgar Hoover had amassed over 17,000 pages of secret information he kept locked in his lifelong and trusted secretary's office. She was Helen Gandy and had been his secretary for 54 years. These private files were not part of the official F.B.I. files. When his domestic employee, James Crawford, found Hoover dead on May 2, 1972, it set off a set of prearranged orders to be followed upon his death. His housekeeper, Annie Fields, called Clyde Tolson, Hoover's number two man in the F.B.I. and a lifelong friend and confidant. Within minutes, Tolson was on the phone to Helen Gandy telling her what to do with the disposition of Hoover's private secret files. Most were destroyed immediately. Some of the secrets about the investigation of the assassination of JFK that the Warren Commission never saw were in those files.

We now know that Hoover was capable of stonewalling information. He once had evidence on his desk that would have cleared a Boston man of murder before he ever stood trial, and yet he let that man be convicted. That man spent almost 30 years in prison before being cleared of the charges. This story is well-documented, with the news show "60 Minutes" running a story on it in 2002.

In that Warren Commission meeting on January 22, 1964, the seven Commission members discussed that it has always been the <u>nature of the F.B.I. to investigate and present the facts, that they do not evaluate, and that they do not make conclusions</u> such as they did about Lee Harvey Oswald being the lone assassin. They also discussed that the F.B.I. had not run out the leads. Instead, the F.B.I. had publicly announced from almost day one that Lee Harvey Oswald was the lone assassin. It is also interesting to note that an F.B.I. secret internal memo issued two days after the assassination, dated Nov 24, 1963, states: "<u>Hoover says Oswald alone did it, Bureau must 'convince the public Oswald is the real Assassin</u>.'" This confidential F.B.I. internal memo two days after the murder of President Kennedy is compelling evidence that something was very wrong inside the F.B.I., as they had not formally entered the investigation yet. The initial investigation was still in the hands of the Dallas Police department 48 hours after the assassination of President Kennedy, on November 24, 1963.

When President Johnson announced that he was going to appoint a commission to investigate the assassination of President Kennedy, F.B.I. Director J. Edgar Hoover was much opposed to such a commission and beside himself, to say it mildly. Any report on the investigation of the assassination of President John F. Kennedy was the Bureau's business, and this was going over Hoover's head.

Hoover did not care for the appointment of Chief Justice Earl Warren to head the commission, and when Warren named J. Lee Rankin as General Counsel for the Commission, Hoover tried to block Rankin's appointment. It was the start of an adversarial relationship between Hoover and the Warren Commission. Hoover ordered dossiers on the members of the Warren Commission and the Commission staff. He also ordered his F.B.I. agents not to volunteer any information to the Warren Commission or its staff. Hoover further ordered that no Bureau official attend the early Warren Commission sessions.

To its credit, the Warren Commission knew up front what they were faced with in dealing with Hoover. In that same early January 22, 1964 Warren Commission meeting, the discussion that day ended with the comment, "They (FBI) would like to have us fold up and quit" and the following discussion.

Boggs: This closes the case, you see, don't you see.
Dulles: Yes I see that.
Rankin: They found the man, there is nothing more to do. The Commission supports their conclusions, and we can go on home and that is the end of it.
Dulles: But that puts the men right on them, if he was not the killer and they employed him, they are it you see. So your argument is correct if they are sure that this is going to close the case, but it don't close the case, they are worse off than ever by doing this.
Boggs: Yes I would think so. And of course, we are even gaining in the realm of speculation. I don't even like for this to be taken down.
Dulles: Yes, I think this record ought to be destroyed. Do you think we need a record of this?

The record was not destroyed; instead, it was discovered years later, but it does give us a glimpse of why the Warren Commission was doomed from the start in finding the truth about the assassination of President John F. Kennedy. One of the things that the Commission members did not know on that January 1964 day, was that Jack Ruby, Oswald's killer, was an informant for the F.B.I. and Hoover had to keep that a secret at all cost. Hoover had spent his life building the prestige and image of the F.B.I., and the fact that the killer of Lee Harvey Oswald was on the F.B.I. payroll as an underworld informant for the F.B.I. and that it might become public, was something J. Edgar Hoover could not bear. It would seriously damage the reputation of the F.B.I. if it became public. This was unthinkable for J. Edgar Hoover as the public might think the F.B.I. had something to do with the assassination. The fact that Jack Ruby was on the F.B.I. payroll as an underworld informant was of no consequence, as we now know. Jack Ruby acted on his own and on impulse only; his killing Oswald had nothing to do with the F.B.I., which I cover in another chapter.

Besides the issues with Hoover, the Warren Commission had its own problems. Contrary to popular belief the seven Warren Commission members were only present at a few of the depositions that were taken, and not all of the members were present at those depositions. A staff of 14 very young lawyers took most of the depositions and did most of the work. These lawyers, as a whole, had very little investigative experience. They were selected by the Justice Department by sending out letters to law professors at some of the nation's law schools and asking the professors to nominate some of their top graduates to be staff members for the commission. The Warren Commission was also under pressure to "Rush to Judgment" as Mark Lane titled one of the first books written, criticizing the final conclusions of the Warren Commission.

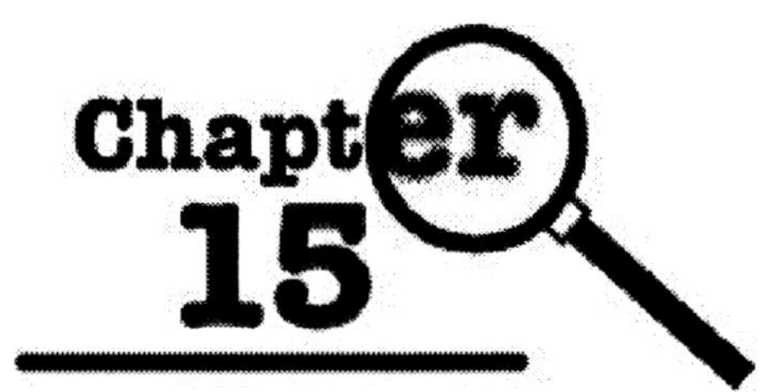

FEBRUARY THRU EARLY JUNE 1964

During the months of February, March, April, and May 1964, the news the public received was much the same. There were articles about who had been called to testify and the assassination was still front-page news. Nevertheless, there was not one article about a missed shot. I had stopped telling anyone about my experience in Dealey Plaza. Due to the constant articles about all three shots hitting into the President's limousine and nothing about a missed shot, whenever I said something about knowing one shot had missed I would get that "oh sure, we know" look that said I don't believe a word you are saying. The fact that I was there and the debris had flown up and hit me in the face was not convincing.

In early May 1964 I made plans to go to the Indianapolis 500. I had grown up on a farm only a few miles from the track and had been to several races. My parents still lived on the farm, about 12 miles from Indianapolis. Before going home, I had bought a movie camera and decided to go back to Dealey Plaza to take some movie pictures so that I could show my parents where I had been during the shooting. On the day of the race in Indianapolis, I took my movie camera with me. We had seats on the front straightway, and on the second lap I had my camera on Jimmy Clark as he sped past and was opening up a wide lead. I heard a gasp from the crowd, and I swung my camera around in time to catch Steve McDonald bounce off the inside wall in flames and start sliding toward me. As McDonald slid across the track in flames toward where I was, I had my camera on him just as race driver Eddie Sachs broad-sided McDonald's car and they both slid to a stop in front of me in flames. Eddie Sachs was killed instantly and Steve McDonald died on the way to the hospital.

In early June there were two articles in the paper that caught my attention. One was that the Warren Commission had announced that they were winding up their investigation and that all three shots had hit into the President's limousine, and the other was about the possibility of a missed shot. I had fully expected to be called before the Warren Commission to testify any day, but it had not happened. Now they were winding up their investigation and ready to publish their findings, though asking questions about the possibility of a missed shot. I thought everybody knew about the missed shot, since the Sheriff's Deputies, the Dallas Police and the F.B.I. had statements from me. So what was going on?

On Friday, June 5, 1964, I was at work talking to a friend and venting my frustration about what I was reading in the papers. I could not believe that the honorable men who made up the Warren Commission could not know that there was indeed a missed shot. My friend, who worked for the DALLAS TIMES HERALD, knew I was sincere. This friend said he was going to tell a TIMES HERALD reporter about me, or better yet, since he was not going to be in the office for a couple of days, he gave me a number to call to ask for a reporter named Jim Lehrer. I called Mr. Lehrer and he was in my office within 30 minutes. We sat in the company meeting room and I told Jim Lehrer what I knew while he took notes. One thing that I required was that he not use my name and Jim Lehrer agreed to that. When we were through talking about the events of November 22, 1963, I asked Jim Lehrer to view the film I had taken at the Indianapolis 500. (I had brought the film and projector to work to show my fellow employees.) I asked Jim Lehrer if it had any commercial value and he replied it did not, saying it was old news and he left. About three hours later, Jim Lehrer called me very excited. He explained that he had written the story about what I had told him and put it on the news wires (the TIMES HERALD was an evening paper and had not come out yet), and he was getting calls from all over wanting to know who I was. Mr. Lehrer said he had kept his word and had not used my name in the article, but he said he had to tell some people in Washington who I was. I told him that was OK, just not to use my name in the local paper. I was to later learn that the F.B.I. was in his office at 4:30 that afternoon interviewing him about the article and what I had observed in Dealey Plaza on November 22, 1963. I have a copy of that F.B.I. report and it is very unflattering. I was portrayed in that report as someone seeking publicity and money even though I had asked that my name not be used in the article.

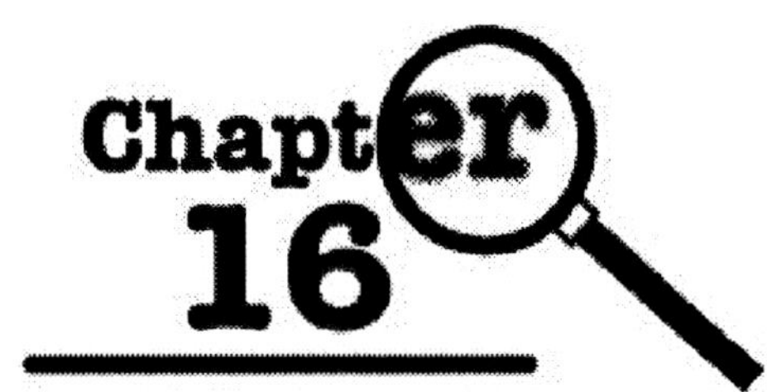

JUNE, JULY 1964

It was years before I was to learn about the effect Jim Lehrer's article had on the Warren Commission and how it altered the final outcome of the Warren Report. Prior to Lehrer's article, many Dealey Plaza witnesses and photographers who had seen and photographed the scar on the curb on November 22, 1963, or the next day, had been called to testify before the Warren Commission. Not one of them was asked about the scar on the curb, nor were they given a chance to volunteer information about the curb mark during their testimony to the Commission. Deputy Sheriff Buddy Walthers was one of those witnesses who had already testified without the missed shot being mentioned in his testimony. When the Warren Commission was faced with the realization that it was now public knowledge that one shot had gone astray, the Commission knew that Mr. Walthers was a witness to the scar on the curb and recalled Mr. Walthers to testify to the facts as he knew them.

It was only a couple of days after the Jim Lehrer article was published on June 5, 1964 in the DALLAS TIMES HERALD that the Warren Commission announced that they were continuing their investigation. Here is a step-by-step account of how the final findings of the Warren Commission were forever altered.

June 5, 1964: The F.B.I. acknowledges that it had interviewed me before and knew about the "claim" of a missed shot.

Early June, 1964: Tom Dillard of the Dallas Morning News made a passing remark at a social function to Assistant U. S. Attorney in Dallas Barefoot Sanders that Dillard had taken pictures of the curb where a missed shot had hit the curb. An associate of Sanders, Martha Jo Stroud, writes J. Lee Rankin, Chief Counsel for the Warren Commission, about the missed shot.

UNITED STATES GOVERNMENT

Memorandum

TO Mr. Belmont

DATE June 8, 1964

FROM A. Rosen

SUBJECT LEE HARVEY OSWALD
IS - R - CUBA
INTERNAL SECURITY

1 - C. D. DeLoach
1 - W. C. Sullivan
(R. E. Lenihan)
1 - I. W. Conrad
1 - Mr. Belmont
1 - Mr. Rosen
1 - Mr. Malley
1 - Mr. Shroder
1 - Mr. Rogge

PURPOSE

To advise the United Press International (UPI) release on 6-5-64, relating to a Dallas auto salesman who reported being hit on the cheek by a ricocheted bullet or piece of curbing is probably identical with Jim Tague, who was interviewed by our Dallas Office on 12-14-63, the results of which have been furnished to the President's Commission.

DETAILS

UPI release dated 6-5-64, relates the "Dallas Times Herald" on 6-5-64, reported an unnamed auto salesman had advised one of the three bullets fired during the assassination apparently hit a curb and he was either hit on the cheek by a ricochet or piece of concrete curb.

The UPI release indicates the salesman asked that his identity be concealed and reports the salesman was by a concrete abutment near the triple overpass adjacent to the Presidential Motorcade at the time of the assassination. The auto salesman indicated he heard three reports which he believed to be shots and on the second shot he felt a sting on his cheek. He maintaine in the following confusion he forgot about it until a policeman told him his face was "bloody." The salesman states he went back to where he had been standing and saw a fresh crease mark on the curb. This incident according to the salesman was reported to a Dallas detective and later to the FBI, who were more concerned "about whether I knew Jack Ruby." The release concludes that the salesman has not been contacted by the Commission.

BACKGROUND

This individual is probably identical with Mr. Jim Tague salesman for the Chuck Hutton Company, Dallas, who was interviewed by our Dallas Office on 12-14-63. The results of this interview

62-109090
RDR:las
(10)

REC 30

64 JUL 13

Memorandum to Mr. Belmont
RE: LEE HARVEY OSWALD

appear on page 31 in the report of SA Robert P. Gemberling dated 12-23-63, captioned as above. This report has been furnished to the Commission.

Tague during interview furnished substantially the same information as reported in the UPI release except it appears he has become more dramatic and has exaggerated the incident in an effort to obtain personal publicity or for other unknown reasons. For example, his interview indicates Tague reported about "two drops of blood" resulted from this incident; however, the UPI release now indicates his face was "bloody." Tague denied knowing Oswald but stated he had been in Ruby's club on a few occasions and knew Ruby by sight; however, denied knowing anything about Ruby's associations.

Based on information developed recently, it is possible that one of the shots fired by Oswald did go wild; however, efforts to locate the portion of curb where a possible shot might have hit has been negative.

ACTION

Since this interview has been reported to the Commission and the UPI release contains substantially the same information developed by our investigation, no further action is recommended.

-2-

June 8, 1964: Under pressure from the press, the F.B.I. makes a second acknowledgement that it had interviewed me in December 1963 and knew all along about the "claim" of a missed shot. The F.B.I. advised United Press International (UPI) that the release on June 5, 1964 relating to a Dallas auto salesman who reported being hit on the cheek by a ricochet bullet or piece of curbing is probably identical with Jim Tague, who was interviewed on December 14, 1963, the results of which have been furnished to the President's Commission.

June 11, 1964: Assistant Counsel Arlen Spector sends a memorandum to General Counsel J. Lee Rankin. "If additional depositions are taken in Dallas, I suggest that Jim Tague, 2424 Inwood, Apartment 253, and Virgie Rackley (Richie), 405 Wood Street be deposed to determine the knowledge of each on where the bullet struck. These two witnesses were mentioned in the early F.B.I. reports, but they have never been deposed."

June 30, 1964: J. Edgar Hoover is sent two photographs, obtained be the Dallas F.B.I. office, of the curb taken by James Underwood of KRLD-TV.

July 2, 1964: The F.B.I. report of Robert Gemberling is released, containing information to the effect that one bullet fired during the assassination went wild, crashing into the curb.

July 7, 1964: J. Edgar Hoover of the F.B.I. received a letter from the President's Commission requesting additional information concerning an alleged mark on the curb in the vicinity of the Schoolbook Depository, Dallas, Texas, which had been photographed by James Underwood, a newsman with KRLD-TV, Dallas, Texas. In connection with this request, the President's Commission letter made available a photograph of the curb made by Tom Dillard of the Dallas Morning News, which had been forwarded by Martha Jo Stroud, Assistant United States Attorney, Dallas, Texas.

July 9, 1964: J. Lee Rankin, General Counsel for the President's Commission (most often referred to as the Warren Commission), mails to me, James T. Tague, a request to appear before the President's Commission for a deposition. (See opposite page.)

July 13, 1964: J. Lee Rankin, General Counsel for the Warren Commission, sends a request to J. Edgar Hoover of the F.B.I. for further investigation of the mark on the curb.

July 15, 1964: A teletype message was sent to J. Edgar Hoover from the Dallas F.B.I. office stating there was no mark to be found.

July 23, 1964: I appear for a deposition to the Warren Commission at the office of the United States Attorney, Dallas, Texas. Arlen Spector was originally named as the member of the staff of the President's Commission authorized to take my deposition; however, Assistant Counsel Wesley J. Liebeler, also a member of the staff, replaced Arlen Spector for the deposition. My full testimony can be found in Volume VII, pages 552 through 558 of the 26-volume Warren Commission findings. The interview for the deposition was polite and to the point, but in the middle of my deposition, Mr. Liebeler said, "Now I understand that you went back there (Dealey Plaza) subsequently and took some pictures of the area, isn't that right?" Stunned at this question out of the blue, I replied, "Pardon?" Mr. Liebeler repeated himself, and I answered, "Yes, about a month ago." Mr. Liebeler then asked, "With a motion picture camera?" I replied, "Yes, I did not know anybody knew about that."

July 24, 1964: The next day, the F.B.I. announces that they have found the mark on the curb.

August 4, 1964: J. Edgar Hoover sends a teletype message to the Dallas F.B.I. office marked "URGENT," and stating "Plans being made to remove a portion of the curb for analysis. [Agent] Lyndal Shaneyfelt will arrive Dallas today and supervise removal."

August 5, 1964: The mark on the curb is photographed by F.B.I. Agent Lyndal Shaneyfelt and then removed from the south side of Main Street, 8 months and 13 days after the assassination of President Kennedy. Yes, the mark was still visible.

PRESIDENT'S COMMISSION
ON THE
ASSASSINATION OF PRESIDENT KENNEDY

200 Maryland Ave. N.E.
Washington, D.C. 20002
Telephone 543-1400

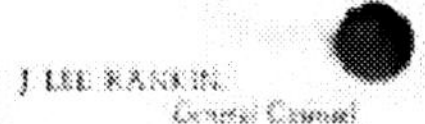
J. LEE RANKIN,
General Counsel

AIR MAIL
REGISTERED
RETURN RECEIPT REQUESTED

JUL 9 1964

Mr. Jim Tague
2424 Inwood
Apartment 253
Dallas, Texas

Dear Mr. Tague:

As you know, this Commission was established by President Johnson on November 29, 1963 to investigate and report upon the facts and circumstances relating to the assassination of our late President, John F. Kennedy, and the subsequent killing of the alleged assassin, Lee Harvey Oswald. Enclosed for your information are copies of Executive Order No. 11130 creating this Commission, Senate Resolution 137 and the Rules of Procedure of this Commission for the taking of testimony.

Mr. Arlen Specter, a member of the Staff of the President's Commission has been authorized by the Commission to take your deposition or affidavit at the office of the United States Attorney, Dallas, Texas, on July 16, 1964 at 11:50 A.M.

It would be helpful if upon receipt of this letter you would confirm your appearance at the hour requested by contacting Mrs. Martha Joe Stroud, Assistant U. S. Attorney, Office of the United States Attorney, Dallas, Texas.

The Commission is authorized to pay your transportation expenses incurred as a result of your appearance before Mr. Specter.

Thank you for your cooperation in the work of the Commission.

Sincerely,

J. Lee Rankin
General Counsel

Enclosures.

F.B.I. REPORT OF AUGUST 5, 1964

The F.B.I. report (Bureau file No. 105-82555) on the opposite page is typical of many F.B.I. reports. A close study of F.B.I. internal reports can be revealing. This F.B.I. report is dated 8/5/64, and is from the Dallas F.B.I. field office and states that "Additional investigation conducted concerning mark on curb on south side of Main Street near triple underpass, which it is alleged was possibly caused by a bullet fired during assassination. No evidence of mark or nick on curb now visible." What makes this report interesting is that while one agent is writing a report that says no mark visible another agent is taking pictures of the mark. 8/5/64 is the same date F.B.I. Agent Shaneyfelt took pictures of the curb mark and had the curb section removed from the street. The pictures that F.B.I. Agent Shaneyfelt took just before the curb section was cut from the street that day reveal that the mark had been patched, but was still visible to the naked eye eight months later.

Another interesting reference in this same report is about, "Photographs taken at Methodist Hospital of Dallas of bone specimen allegedly from the skull of President Kennedy obtained." The bone specimen referred to was a very large piece of the rear of President Kennedy's skull found near a curb on Elm Street a few minutes after the assassination and immediately taken to Methodist Hospital. There is no evidence that the Warren Commission ever viewed this large bone specimen from the rear of President Kennedy's skull or viewed pictures of this large bone specimen. The official autopsy report does not reveal a piece of skull is missing from the back of President Kennedy's head. This one vital piece of evidence, the fact that a large piece of occipital bone from the rear Of President Kennedy's head was blown out, was proof that at least one shot came from in front of the President, thus more than one shooter, and a conspiracy. This large piece of skull from the back of President Kennedy's head and the pictures taken of this piece of skull did eventually wind up in the National Archives. The Piece of skull has disappeared from the Archives, but the pictures remain.

Another point of interest in all the F.B.I. reports is the subject title. They are headed, "LEE HARVEY OSWALD – INTERNAL SECURITY – RUSSIA – CUBA. The fact that Internal Security, Russia, and Cuba are included with Lee Harvey Oswald's name is intriguing. I can understand Internal Security, but the meaning behind the F.B.I. still including Russia and Cuba in the subject heading's eight months after the assassination raises questions.

UNITED STATES DEPARTMENT OF JUSTICE
FEDERAL BUREAU OF INVESTIGATION

Copy to:

Report of: ROBERT P. GEMBERLING Office: DALLAS
Date: 8/5/64

Field Office File No.: DL 100-10461 Bureau File No.: 105-82555

Title: LEE HARVEY OSWALD

Character: INTERNAL SECURITY - RUSSIA - CUBA

Synopsis:

CLOTILE WILLIAMS heard assassination shots while standing on northwest corner of Houston and Elm Streets, Dallas, Texas, but did not see anything that aroused her suspicion and did not know from where the shots came. Supplemental listing of exhibits by item number and description prepared. Additional investigation conducted concerning mark on curb on south side of Main Street near triple underpass, which it is alleged was possibly caused by bullet fired during assassination. No evidence of mark or nick on curb now visible. Photographs taken of location where mark once appeared, together with other photographs reflecting angle of such location in relation to the sixth floor window of the Texas School Book Depository (TSBD) from which assassination shots fired. Photographs also taken from inside sixth floor of TSBD southeast corner window from which assassination shots fired, showing distance between floor and window sill and height of opening in the window when window half open. Photographs taken of person approximate height of OSWALD showing relative position of window ledge and window to such person. Photographs taken at Methodist Hospital of Dallas of bone specimen allegedly from skull of President KENNEDY obtained. Additional investigation conducted with negative results concerning claim by Mrs. EDITH WHITWORTH that she directed OSWALD family to Irving Sports Shop, Irving, Texas, in early November 1963, which investigation consisted of interviews of certain parents of female babies born 10/20/63, in the Irving and Dallas, Texas, area to determine if they were the individuals

August 5, 1964: The curb is given a preliminary analysis and found to have a slight lead residue where the bullet hit the curb.

August 6, 1964: The curb section is received by the F.B.I. laboratory.

August 10, 1964: The mark on the curb is given a spectrographic analysis in the F.B.I. laboratory.

August 12, 1964: F.B.I. Director J. Edgar Hoover sends a letter by courier to Warren Commission General Counsel J. Lee Rankin. In part, it reads: "Reference is made to your letter July 7, 1964. This mark was located and was found to be 23 feet, 4 inches from the abutment of the triple underpass. This mark corresponds with photographs taken by James Underwood and Tom Dillard. Small foreign metal smears were found adhering to the curbing section within the area of the mark. These metal smears were spectrographically determined to be essentially lead with a trace of antimony. No copper was found." (The fact that Hoover's letter states "No copper was found" has significant meaning and will be covered in a later chapter.)

The Warren Commission quickly concluded that one bullet did in fact go wild and missed the President's limousine completely, striking the curb near me. The single bullet theory is adopted by the Warren Commission, that one bullet hit both President Kennedy and Governor Connally, and that one bullet hit the President in the head.

September 24, 1964: The President's Commission on the Assassination of President Kennedy submits its final report to President Johnson.

It was also announced that all documents concerning the assassination of President Kennedy would be sealed for 75 years. My dear friend Harold Weisberg changed that when he sued the United States Justice Department and the Federal Bureau of Investigation under the Freedom of Information Act. Harold Weisberg's lawsuit resulted in the F.B.I. assassination documents being released, and once these documents were released in 1977 and 1978, it took hours upon hours to sift through the thousands and thousands of released documents. These documents and F.B.I. reports are revealing and tell a story of their own about the investigation. The F.B.I. interview with me on December 14, 1963 was included in an early report to the Warren Commission on December 23, 1963. My report of a missed shot, a shot that went wild, apparently fell through the cracks with the Warren Commission because there was no follow up report to the Commission by the F.B.I. as to the missed shot. What we do know now from the released documents was that the F.B.I. did in fact follow up on my report of a missed shot and verified that there was a missed shot, but never said another word nor did they make another report to the Warren Commission about a missed shot. The Jim Lehrer article appeared, which did not contain my name at my request, in the DALLAS TIMES HERALD on June 5, 1964, revealing to the public for the first time that there was a missed shot. F.B.I. documents reveal that they knew immediately that the article was about me, James T. Tague, and F.B.I. agents were in Jim Lehrer's office that afternoon. The F.B.I. report made from that interview with Jim Lehrer was demeaning to me as someone seeking money and publicity, indicating the F.B.I. knew about my "claim" of a missed shot from a December 1963 interview with me, and that no further action should be taken.

The F.B.I. documents that were supposed to be sealed for 75 years tell a different story. The F.B.I. had indeed investigated my "claim" of a missed shot and knew the "claim" was true, one shot went wild and hit the curb near me. The F.B.I. knew where the bullet had hit the curb and they knew who took pictures of the mark on the curb. That day, June 5, 1964, when Jim Lehrer put the story on the U.P.I. news release and before the DALLAS TIMES HERALD story hit the streets of Dallas, the Dallas F.B.I. office sent a teletype to J. Edgar Hoover. The teletype read: "The Dallas F.B.I. office would obtain a copy of photograph from KRLD-TV where a mark appeared on a curb and was in close proximity to the place where auto salesman claimed he was standing." The F.B.I. knew all along where a missed shot had hit the curb (close proximity to where I was standing) and knew who had taken a picture of the mark and where to go get a copy of that picture (KRLD-TV). Another report by airmail to J. Edgar Hoover on June 16, 1964 verifies the same. That the F.B.I. had not revealed any further information about a missed shot to the Warren Commission, other than an initial interview in December 1963, is stunning; they knew that an auto salesman's "claim" of a missed shot was correct. The F.B.I. was not through, however, because when asked by the Warren Commission to find where the bullet had hit the curb, the F.B.I. replied back to the Warren Commission that they could not find any place where a bullet had hit the curb. Under pressure from J. Lee Rankin, Chief Counsel for the Warren Commission, and with additional pictures taken of the curb, the F.B.I. suddenly found where the bullet had hit the curb the day after I testified in July 1964 before the Warren Commission. Pictures taken of the curb on August 5, 1964, and before the curb section was cut from the street that day, reveal the bullet mark had been patched, but was still visible to the naked eye after eight and one half months.

That I was observed taking pictures in Dealey Plaza in May 1964, that the film then disappeared from my home, that the bullet mark had been patched before it was cut from the street, that the F.B.I. withheld information about the missed shot from the Warren Commission, that the F.B.I. pretended to not be able to find the bullet mark when they knew where it was all along raises some serious questions about the integrity of J. Edgar Hoover in the investigation of the assassination of President John F. Kennedy.

Shaneyfelt Exhibit No. 26

UNITED STATES DEPARTMENT OF JUSTICE

FEDERAL BUREAU OF INVESTIGATION

In Reply, Please Refer to
File No.

July 17, 1964
Dallas, Texas

LEE HARVEY OSWALD

By letter dated July 7, 1964, the President's Commission requested additional investigation concerning an alleged mark on the curb in the vicinity of the Texas School Book Depository (TSBD), Dallas, Texas, which had been photographed by James Underwood, a Newsman with KRLD-TV, Dallas, Texas. In connection with this request, the President's Commission letter made available a photograph of the curb made by Tom Dillard of "The Dallas Morning News" which had been forwarded to the President's Commission by Martha Joe Stroud, Assistant United States Attorney, Dallas, Texas.

On July 15, 1964, James Underwood, residence, 9751 Parkford Drive, Dallas, Texas, a Newsman for KRLD-TV, Dallas, was shown two photographs. One of these photographs is of a mark on the curb on the south side of Main Street near the triple underpass and shows a hand shielding the light from this mark. The second photograph was taken looking across Main Street and up Elm Street toward the TSBD. Mr. Underwood identified these photographs as frames taken from a 16 mm movie film, which film was taken by him on the morning of November 23, 1963. Mr. Underwood advised he had been told by a Deputy Sheriff, whose name he could not recall, that there was a mark on the curb on the south side of Main Street near the underpass, which was possibly made by a ricocheting bullet. The photograph of the hand shielding the mark on the curb was made by Underwood squatting down in the gutter to get a close-up view of the mark, and the picture of the TSBD was taken by placing the handle attached to the underneath side of Underwood's movie camera on the curb near the mark and pointing the camera back toward the TSBD, in order to get a low-level shot.

Mr. Underwood repeated what he had told Federal Bureau of Investigation Agents on June 11, 1964, that he could not be positive the mark was made by a ricocheting bullet, but appeared to him that it could have been, based on knowledge acquired by him while in the military service. He further stated it was definitely a mark on the curb and not a nick in the curb. He repeated that the concrete was not broken and that the mark appeared to have possibly been made recently, but he could not judge how much time had passed since the mark was made when he took the photographs of it.

CD 1385a

LEE HARVEY OSWALD

Mr. Underwood stated that prior to taking the photographs he met Tom Dillard, a Photographer for "The Dallas Morning News," near the entrance to the Dallas County Jail, and had told Dillard about the information he had received from the Deputy Sheriff about the mark on the curb. Dillard indicated he would possibly also take a still photograph of this mark.

On July 15, 1964, Tom C. Dillard, residence, 7022 Merrilee Lane, Dallas, Texas, a Photographer for "The Dallas Morning News," advised that on the morning of November 23, 1963, while at the Dallas County Jail entrance, he had received information from James Underwood, a Newsman for KRLD-TV, to the effect there was a mark on the curb on the south side of Main Street near the triple underpass. Underwood had told Dillard that the mark was possibly made by a bullet. Later during the afternoon of November 23, 1963, Dillard, using a Mamiyaflex 120 Camera, took a picture of a mark on the curb on the south side of Main Street about twenty feet east of the triple underpass. Dillard stated he was of the opinion the mark very possibly could have been made by a ricocheting bullet and that it had been recently made.

Mr. Dillard was shown a photograph of a mark on the curb with a hand holding a pencil pointing toward the mark. He identified this photograph as a copy of the one he had taken on the afternoon of November 23, 1963.

Mr. Dillard stated he definitely recalls it was a mark on the curb rather than a nick in the curb and the concrete was not broken or chipped.

On July 15, 1964, two Special Agents of the Federal Bureau of Investigation, accompanied by Tom C. Dillard, a Photographer for "The Dallas Morning News," and James Underwood, a Newsman for KRLD-TV, went to the area approximately twenty feet east of the triple underpass and on the south side of Main Street. Through the use of the same camera used by Mr. Underwood on November 23, 1963, and by aligning three reference points in a photograph of the TSBD taken by Mr. Underwood on November 23, 1963, from this same area, it was ascertained the mark observed and photographed by Mr. Underwood and Mr. Dillard had been at a point on the curb twenty-one feet and eleven and one-half inches east of a point where Main Street passes under the triple underpass. This same point where the mark had been observed by Mr. Underwood and Mr. Dillard was seventy-three feet and five inches west of the first lamp post on the south side of Main Street, which lamp post is the first one located east from the triple underpass on Main Street.

- 2 -

LEE HARVEY OSWALD

The area on the curb from this point for a distance of ten feet in either direction was carefully checked and it was ascertained there was no nick in the curb in the checked area, nor was any mark observed.

Reference points in the photograph taken by Mr. Underwood used to locate this point were a lamp post located in the right of the photograph, which appears to be midway between two buildings, a lamp post located on the north side of Elm Street, which is in line with the third row of windows from the southwest corner of the TSBD, and which face south, and a traffic sign located on the left side of the photograph, which is to the west of the TSBD.

It should be noted that no nick or break in the concrete was observed, in the area checked, nor was there any mark similar to the one in the photographs taken by Underwood and Dillard observed in the area checked either by the Special Agents, by Mr. Underwood, or by Mr. Dillard. It should be noted that, since this mark was observed on November 23, 1963, there have been numerous rains, which could have possibly washed away such a mark and also that the area is cleaned by a street cleaning machine about once a week, which would also wash away any such mark.

- 3 -

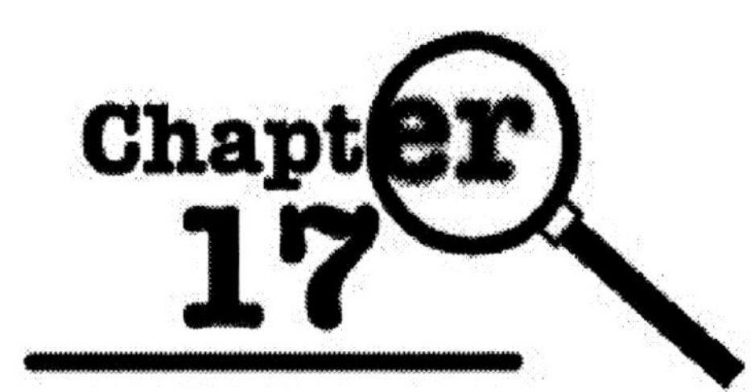

THE PRESIDENTS COMMISSION ON THE ASSASSINATION OF PRESIDENT KENNEDY

AKA THE WARREN REPORT

On November 29, 1963, President Lyndon Johnson authorized Executive Order 11130, an Executive order creating a Commission to ascertain, evaluate, and report upon the facts relating to the assassination of the late President John F. Kennedy and the subsequent violent death of the man charged with the assassination and S.J. Res, 137, 88th Congress, a concurrent resolution, conferring upon the Commission the power to administer oaths and affirmations, examine witnesses, receive evidence, and issue subpoenas. The Commission soon evolved as follows.

Chief Justice Earl Warren, Chairman

Senator Richard R. Russell
Representative Gerald R. Ford
Senator John Sherman Cooper
Mr. Allen W. Dulles
Representative Hale Boggs
Mr. John J. McCloy

J. Lee Rankin, General Counsel
Assistant Counsel

Francis W. H. Adams
Joseph A. Ball
David W. Belin
William T. Coleman, Jr.
Melvin Aron Eisonberg
Burt W. Griffen
Leon D. Hubert, Jr.
Albert E. Jenner, Jr.
Wesley J. Liebeler
Norman Redlich
W. David Slawson
Arlen Spector
Samuel A. Stern
Howard P. Willens

STAFF MEMBERS

Philip Barson, Edward A. Conroy, John Hart Ely, Alfred Goldberg, Murry J. Laulight, Arthur Marmor, Richard M. Mosk, John J. O'Brien, Stuart Pollak, AlfreddaScorey, Charles N. Shaffer, Jr.

On September 24, 1964, the President's Commission on the Assassination of President Kennedy, better known as the Warren Commission, sent its final report to President Johnson. Their conclusions were:

* There was no credible evidence of any conspiracy.
* Lee Harvey Oswald acted alone in killing President Kennedy.
* Lee Harvey Oswald acted alone in killing officer J. D. Tippit.
* Jack Ruby acted alone to kill Lee Harvey Oswald.
* All the shots came from the sixth floor window of the Schoolbook Depository where a rifle owned by Oswald was discovered.
* Three shots were fired.
* The first shot passed through Kennedy's back/neck and then through the chest and wrist of Governor Connally.
* The second shot hit President Kennedy in the head.
* The third shot missed.

The case was closed, and the press as well as the American people accepted the report with enthusiasm and admiration. There was hardly a word of dissent, just praise for the great job the Commission had done. Their findings were accepted as the full truth. The initial report contained nearly 900 pages with over 6,000 footnotes. The Commission reported that the F.B.I. conducted 25,000 interviews and the C.I.A. another 1,550. The general public had a sense of relief that a "lone nut gunman" had acted alone and there was no conspiracy.

A few weeks later the full 26-volume report was released containing 20,000 pages and over 10 million words. The 26 volumes were poorly indexed and it was evident that it would take researchers years to match testimony and evidence. The voluminous mishmash of evidence in the 26 volumes was almost impossible to match with testimony. There was no logical way to match the testimony to the exhibits; items were not classified or indexed and were chaotic and incomplete. Some witnesses had been cut off in mid-sentence while trying to relate what they had witnessed, and the questions asked of some of the witnesses seemed to follow a pattern to fit preconceived conclusions. Important questions were still unanswered, and evidence was overlooked that would impede the final findings. It was not long before the initial praise of the report turned to skepticism as researchers poured over the full 26 volumes. It started with suspicions in the foreign press that the Warren Report had left too many important questions unanswered. A few articles of doubt and deceit about the Warren Report started appearing in magazines and books. One of the earliest critics was former Senate Investigator Harold Weisberg who wrote a series of books called WHITEWASH. Harold had to publish his books privately as no establishment publisher would touch them. Some of the other early books were RUSH TO JUDGMENT by Mark Lane, INQUEST by Edward J. Epstein, ACCESSORIES AFTER THE FACT by Sylvia Meagher, and THE UNANSWERED QUESTIONS ABOUT PRESIDENT KENNEDY'S ASSASSINATION by Sylvan Fox. The establishment media, however, especially the newspapers, still expressed faith in the Warren Report.

FROM THE INITIAL REPORT

Seconds after the President's car turned off Houston onto Elm, shots sounded in rapid succession. The President's hands moved to his neck. He appeared to stiffen for a moment, then lurched slightly forward in his seat. A bullet had entered the base of the back of the neck slightly to the right of his spine. It traversed downward and exited from the front of the neck, causing a nick in the left lower portion of the knot in the President's necktie. Before the shooting started, Governor Connally had been facing toward the crowd on the right. He started to turn toward the left and suddenly felt a blow on his back. The governor had been hit by a bullet that entered at the extreme right side of his back at a point below his right armpit. The bullet traveled through his chest in a downward and forward direction, exiting below his right nipple, passing through his right wrist, which had been in his lap, and then caused a wound to his left thigh. The force of the bullet's impact appeared to spin the Governor to his right, and Mrs. Connally pulled him down to her lap. Another bullet then struck President Kennedy in the rear portion of his head, causing a massive and fatal head wound. The President fell to the left into Mrs. Kennedy's lap.

At the scene of the shooting, there was evident confusion at the outset concerning the point of origin of the shots. Witnesses differed in their accounts of the direction from which the sound of the shots emanated. Within a few minutes, attention was centered on the Texas Schoolbook Depository.

When the shots were fired, a Dallas motorcycle patrolman, Marrion I. Baker, was riding in the motorcade at a point several cars behind the President. He saw pigeons scattering in the air from their perches on the Schoolbook Depository Building and raced his motorcycle to the building, pushing his way through the spectators toward the entrance. There he encountered Roy Truly, the building superintendent, who offered Baker his help. They dashed up the stairs, and when they reached the second-floor landing, Mr. Baker thought he caught a glimpse of someone in the lunchroom. Gun in hand, he rushed in and saw a man about 20 feet away walking toward the other end of the lunchroom.

The man was empty-handed. At Baker's command, the man turned and approached him. Truly, who had started up the stairs to the third floor, returned to see what had delayed the patrolman. Baker asked Truly whether he knew this man. Truly replied that the man was Lee Harvey Oswald and he worked in the building, whereupon Baker turned from the man and proceeded up the stairs with Truly.

About a minute later, Oswald was seen passing through the second floor offices with a coke in his hand. At approximately 12:40 P.M., Oswald boarded a bus at a point on Elm Street seven short blocks east of the Depository building. Mary Bledsoe, a former landlady, was on the bus and recognized him. A few minutes later, Oswald exited the bus as it was stuck in traffic and caught a taxi to his room at 1026 N. Beckley Street. Mrs. Earlene Roberts, his housekeeper, was surprised to see him as it was about 1 P.M. Mrs. Roberts remarked to him that he seemed to be in quite a hurry. A few minutes later Oswald emerged from his room and rushed out of the house.

About 45 minutes after the assassination, another violent shooting occurred in Dallas. The victim was Patrolman J. D. Tippit of the Dallas Police Department. He was shot about 9/10ths of a mile from Oswald's boarding house, and witnesses said the gunman fit Oswald's description. A few short minutes and a few blocks away, Oswald was seen entering the Texas Theater. When confronted in the theater, Oswald pulled a pistol from his waist; there was a scuffle, and he was quickly subdued and taken into custody.

Meanwhile the Dallas Police had been searching the Depository and found a sniper's nest and three spent cartridges on the sixth floor. A few moments later, an Italian-made 6.5 caliber rifle was found. At about the same time, the Building Superintendent, Roy Truly, informed the police that the only employee missing was Lee Harvey Oswald.

When Lee Harvey Oswald was brought into the Dallas Police Station at about 2 P.M., November 22, 1964, for the shooting of Officer Tippit, he was quickly connected to the assassination of President Kennedy and the wounding of Governor Connally. That evening he was paraded before reporters and public television. The rifle was quickly connected to him, indicating he was the man, the lone assassin. Witnesses at the scene of the assassination had seen a rifle in the sixth floor window of the Schoolbook Depository. A nearly whole bullet that had fallen off a stretcher at Parkland hospital and two bullet fragments found in the President's limousine were matched to the rifle found on the sixth floor to the exclusion of all other weapons. The three spent cartridges found on the sixth floor were matched to the same rifle. The inside surface of the windshield of the President's limousine was cracked but not penetrated. The nature of the bullet wounds to President Kennedy and Governor Connally established that the shots were fired from above and behind the Presidential limousine. There was no credible evidence that the shots were fired from anywhere else. The weight of the evidence indicates there were three shots fired. One shot hit both Kennedy and Connally, one shot hit Kennedy in the head, and one shot missed, hit the curbing near James T. Tague and sprayed debris into Tague's face. The shots that killed President Kennedy and injured Governor Connally were fired by Lee Harvey Oswald. Oswald killed Officer Tippit about 45 minutes after the assassination. Jack Ruby killed Oswald two days later as Oswald was being transferred to the Dallas County jail. Deficiencies of the Dallas Police contributed to the killing of Oswald. There was no evidence that Oswald or Ruby were part of any conspiracy. There was no credible evidence that Ruby and Oswald knew each other or that Oswald knew Officer Tippit. There was no evidence of a conspiracy, subversion, or disloyalty to the United States Government by any Federal, State, or local official. Lee Harvey Oswald was a lone nut assassin who acted alone. The public accepted this report.

Shortly after the condensed, single volume, 900-page report was published, the complete report consisting of everything that had come before the Warren Commission was published. It was 26 volumes, measuring 35 inches across when the volumes are put side by side. About half the information in the 26 volumes is about Oswald's and Ruby's backgrounds. There is page after page of copies of Lee and Marina Oswald's personal papers that contributes nothing to the investigation. The same thing can be said about the investigation of Jack Ruby's background. The other half is depositions taken from witnesses. Few of the witnesses actually appeared before the seven-member Warren Commission; most depositions were taken by one of the 14 Assistant Counsel lawyers. There are photographs of the evidence that was collected, the gun, shell casings, the President's shirt and coat, photos of Oswald in the Marines, etc. The autopsy results are represented by drawings that do not match the known facts. The Federal Bureau of Investigation reportedly did 25,000 interviews during the investigation, but only submitted 9,000 reports to the Warren Commission. Lacking from the 26-volume report is what leads were followed other than Lee Harvey Oswald. Also lacking from the 26 volumes is J. Edgar Hoover's 5-volume F.B.I. report submitted on December 9, 1963.

LEE HARVEY OSWALD

It is evident in the 26 volumes that the F.B.I. did an intensive background check of Lee Harvey Oswald. He was born in New Orleans, and at age three, he was placed in an orphanage. Taken out of the orphanage at age four by his mother and moved to Dallas, his mother remarried for the third time. Oswald started first grade in Benbrook, Texas. In Benbrook, his mother separated from her third husband and Lee had to restart the first grade in Covington, Louisiana. While he was still in first grade, the family moved back to Fort Worth, Texas for his mother's reconciliation with her husband. At age eight, his mother divorced her third husband. For the next five and a half years, Lee's school record in Fort Worth was average. At age 12, his mother moved the family to New York City, and the next year and a half in New York was marked by Lee's refusal to attend school and by emotional and psychological problems. Lee underwent psychiatric study at the Youth House where he was diagnosed as "seriously detached, and withdrawn", and it was noted on his medical records, "A rather pleasant, appealing quality about this emotionally starved, affectionate youngster. He experiences fantasies about power, hurting people, but not a behavior problem. He appears withdrawn and evasive, a boy who prefers to spend time alone." He tested above average in intelligence. His mother denied Lee further psychiatric assistance and he returned to school where his grades and attendance temporarily improved. In 1954, at age 14, while Lee's case was still pending in court, his mother and Lee left for New Orleans, the city of Lee's birth. Upon his return to New Orleans, Lee maintained mediocre grades and had no behavior problems. Neighbors and others who knew him outside of school remembered him as a quiet, solitary and introverted boy who read a great deal and whose vocabulary made him quite articulate. At 16, Lee dropped out of school and tried to join the Marines, but was rejected because of his age. Lee worked at odd jobs during the next few months and started to read communist literature, occasionally praised communism, and expressed a desire to join the communist party. Another move followed in July 1956, when Lee and his mother returned to Fort Worth. Lee reentered high school, dropped out after a few weeks and enlisted in the Marine Corps on October 24, 1956, six days after his 17th birthday. In basic training with an M-1 rifle, Lee scored a rating of "sharpshooter" on a marksman/ sharpshooter/expert scale. Lee received training in aviation fundamentals and radar scanning. Most of those who knew him in the Marines described him as a loner who resented authority. He was court-martialed once for possessing an unregistered privately-owned weapon and on another occasion for using provocative language to a non-commissioned officer. He was, however, generally able to comply with Marine discipline. Oswald served 15 months overseas, most of it in Japan. His final year was spent at Santa Ana, California. While in the Marines, Oswald studied the Russian language. Lee was discharged from the Marines on September 11, 1959. and he returned to Fort Worth, where he remained with his mother three days and left for New Orleans. In New Orleans, he booked passage to Le Havre, France and sailed on September 20, 1959. On October 16, 1959, Oswald arrived in Moscow by train after crossing the border from Finland, having secured a visa for a six-day stay in the Soviet Union. He immediately applied for Soviet citizenship. On the afternoon of October 21, 1959, Oswald was ordered to leave the Soviet Union by 8 P.M. that evening. That afternoon, in an apparent suicide attempt, Oswald slashed his wrist. After being released from the hospital, Oswald appeared at the American Embassy and stated he wished to renounce his American citizenship so he could become a Russian citizen. The Soviet government did not grant his request, but in January 1960 he was given permission to remain in the Soviet Union on a year-to-year basis. He was sent to Minsk where he worked in a radio factory as an unskilled laborer. In January 1961, his permission to remain in the Soviet Union was extended for another year. In February 1961, he wrote the American embassy in Moscow expressing a desire to return to the United States. In March 1961, Oswald met a 19-year-old Russian girl named Marina Nikolaevna Prusakova, a pharmacist, who had been brought up in Leningrad but was then living with an aunt and uncle in Minsk. They were married on April 30, 1961. Oswald then corresponded with American and Soviet authorities seeking approval for him and his wife to depart for the United States. Lee Oswald and his wife Marina and new child traveled from Russia to the United States in June 1962 and they settled in Fort Worth, Texas where they were met by a group of Russian-born or Russian-speaking persons who lived in the Dallas/Fort Worth area. These people were very generous to the Oswalds, giving them gifts, food, clothing, baby furniture, and arranging appointments and transportation for medical and dental treatment. When Oswald started looking for employment in October 1962 and when there were marital difficulties, Marina and their child stayed with various members of this group. Oswald's relationship with the Russian community was strained, and he resented the help the "Russian friends" gave to Marina and the child. On April 10, 1963, Lee Harvey Oswald took a shot at resigned Major General Edwin A. Walker; the shot missed. Two weeks later, Oswald went to New Orleans and was later joined by Marina and their daughter. Marina was pregnant with their second child. In late September 1963, Ruth Paine drove to New Orleans and brought Marina and the child back to Irving, Texas because the Oswald's were still having marital difficulties. Soon after Marina left New Orleans, Oswald went to Mexico City and visited the Russian Embassy. Oswald then returned to Dallas, rented a room, and got a job at the Schoolbook Depository on October 15, 1963.

THE LULL BEFORE THE STORM

When the condensed Warren Report was published in late 1964, I bought a copy and read it with interest. I was amazed at all the information the Warren Commission had gathered, and I was impressed with the investigation and their findings. I was glad to see that the missed shot that hit near me was at last acknowledged by the Warren Commission and in the report. I had a problem though understanding the F.B.I. laboratory spectrographic analysis results on the curb, that there was lead and antimony found where the bullet had hit, but no trace of copper, such as was on the bullet found on the floor at Parkland Hospital. The report went on to say that since no copper was found, whatever hit the curb had to have been a fragment of a bullet. When I saw that scar on the curb right after the assassination of President Kennedy, the scar was at least a half-inch wide and three quarters of an inch long and surely made by a whole bullet. I had to remind myself that the F.B.I. does not make mistakes, that they know what they are doing and if they say something you can take it to the bank. I thought to myself at the time, it must have been a very large fragment, most of the entire bullet in fact, to have done the damage that it did to the curb. I reasoned that my growing up with a rifle in my hand and target shooting under the bridge and seeing the marks on concrete from my rifle shots did not make me an expert on ballistics. J. Edgar Hoover and his F.B.I. agents were the experts and I accepted the F.B.I.'s findings and put the assassination of President John F. Kennedy out of my mind.

I believe it was in early 1966 that I got a letter in the mail asking me to call a phone number in Arlington, Texas. I called the number, finding it was a motel, and I asked for the person who had signed the letter. I was soon connected to the writer of the letter. The man who had answered my call explained to me that he would pay me $200 to answer a few questions about what I had witnessed during the assassination of President Kennedy. At that time I was naïve and did not think anything other than that I could use the money. This man, and I cannot remember his name, gave me an address and a time to be there. When I got to the motel and knocked on the door, I was invited in and noticed that a camera had been set up. The man that I had talked to introduced me to a man named Mark Lane. Mr. Lane explained that he wanted to ask me a few questions and film my answers. I was skeptical, but agreed to it. Mr. Lane asked me several questions with the camera on me and then asked the same questions with the camera on him. I remember asking how that was going to work and I was told that when they edited the film they would match Mr. Lane's questions with my answers. I left there thinking that I hoped they matched the right questions to the right answers and that I did not want to do anymore private interviews. To this day, 30 some years later, I have not seen this interview.

By this time, 1966, some controversy was beginning over the Warren Commission's conclusions. Several magazines had articles that raised questions and a few books critical of the Warren Commission were being published. I bought and saved these magazines and books. I tried to read some of the books, and after a chapter or two, I would find something I knew was not exactly true and I would put the book or article aside. The assassination of President Kennedy was not one of my priorities and I was not consumed by what had happened in front of my eyes on November 22, 1963. I did feel, however, that saving these articles and books for my grandchildren would be a nice thing to do.

I was at work one day when I got a call from a man who identified himself as Jimmy Kerr. It was now over four years since the assassination of President Kennedy. Jimmy Kerr was a Dallas reporter with many local police and sheriff's office connections. I first met Jimmy in January 1968, when he wanted to interview me for a story he was doing on the Kennedy Assassination. I, at first, turned him down. I had recently done an interview that I did not care for the way it been done and had decided not to do any more interviews. Jimmy was persistent, however, calling me three or four times offering me $350 for an hour of my time, and I repeatedly turned him down. Jimmy was a good talker though and I did finally agree. We did the interview and Jimmy took notes. He also wanted a picture of me standing in Dealey Plaza at the same spot I was in at the time of the President's assassination. After the picture was taken Jimmy pulled out a piece of paper for me to sign that said he could use my interview and picture in his story. I quickly scanned the piece of paper and signed it without giving much thought to it. A couple of months later, while at work one day, a fellow employee approached me and stated, "That is quite an article you wrote for the National Enquirer on the Kennedy Assassination."

I replied, "What article? I didn't write any article for the National Enquirer." He said, "Well, your name is on it as the author and it contains your picture."

I went straight to the nearest 7-11 and bought a copy of the National Enquirer (see next page), and there on the April 7, 1968 issue of the National Enquirer was a screaming front page headline that took up half of the front page, MAN WOUNDED IN ASSASSINATION OF JFK FINNALLY TALKS, with a sub-headline: "A few minutes after the shooting, while blood was streaming down my face, I showed police the mark on the curb where a bullet or bullet fragment hit near me." It was a five-page article, and had my picture in it along with President Kennedy's and Governor Connally's pictures. The article was full of stretched quotes and many exaggerations. The sub-headline about blood streaming down my face was a total fabrication; there was never blood streaming down my face, and I had never made that statement. I only had a few drops of blood on my face from being peppered by the debris from a missed shot. The article was signed JAMES TAGUE as if I had personally written it. It did not take me long to put together that this was the result of the Jimmy Kerr interview. I was initially very upset with Mr. Kerr, but wound up being very good friends with Jimmy for many years. I found out years later that Jimmy had been paid a large fee for this story, but by then I could laugh about it. Through the years Jimmy would call me and say, "Hey, mystery man, what's going on?"

You could usually find Jimmy hanging around Dallas County Sheriff Bill Decker's office, and Jimmy always had a lot of inside information about what was going on around the town. It was fun and interesting to hear his stories. One of his stories, that I believe to be true, was about him going to the Dallas Police Station the evening of the assassination and walking into the property room. The door was open and no one was there as they were all over in another section of the police station watching Oswald being paraded before reporters. There were articles laid out on the counter that had been taken from the garage in Irving where Marina Oswald had been living with the Paines. There were also some duplicated photos laying on the counter and Jimmy helped himself to a copy of each.

Another story I believe to be true from Jimmy was about the official photographs that were taken of the sniper's nest on the sixth floor of the Schoolbook Depository. According to Jimmy, the official photographs that we see today were not taken on Friday shortly after the assassination, but were taken on Monday, three days after the assassination. Jimmy maintained that the officials had arranged the boxes and spent shell casings as they felt they would look best for the official pictures. The Warren Commission exhibits seem to confirm that Jimmy knew what he was talking about. Commission Exhibits 509, 724, and 733 are supposed to be of the snipers nest, but they show three different versions of the boxes stacked around the sniper's nest.

NATIONAL ENQUIRER 15¢

Vol. 42, No. 31, April 7, 1968

Whatever Happened to The Dead End Kids?

EXCLUSIVE

MAN WOUNDED IN ASSASSINATION OF JFK FINALLY TALKS

A few minutes after the shooting, while blood was still streaming from the wound in my face, I showed police the mark on a curb where a bullet or bullet fragment hit near me. (Continued in centerfold)

DOUBLE BOOK BONUS:

Rock 'n' Roll Causes Serious Hearing Loss

How You Can Beat the Blues When Depression Sets In

FINGERED AS MARTIN LUTHER KING'S ASSASSIN

It was nearly 10 years after Jimmy Kerr's National Enquirer article appeared that I learned that the article had resulted in my being fingered as Martin Luther King's assassin. Harold Weisberg called me one evening shortly after he had received thousands of FBI documents on the Kennedy and King assassinations from the government. Harold had spent years battling the U.S. Government under the Freedom of Information Act for release of these FBI documents. A group of nearby college students from Hood College had volunteered to help him sort through these documents and file them in an orderly fashion in his basement in more than 60 four-drawer filing cabinets. In that call to me, Harold was almost laughing as he told me he was mailing me something I would get a kick out of. I kept trying to get Harold to tell me what it was and he kept telling me no, he was going to mail it to me. A few days later, I received his mail. Enclosed were five pages of FBI reports concerning the Martin Luther King Assassination dated 4/7/68, with James Tague named as a suspect in the assassination. Two men, Billy Northern and Sidney Joiner, had read the National Inquirer article of 4/7/68 at a bus station in West Memphis, Arkansas and saw my picture in the Inquirer. They determined that my picture in the National Inquirer matched a description and sketch of King's Assassin that had appeared in the Memphis Commercial Appeal newspaper on 4/6/68. Northern and Joiner then went to the Commercial Appeal newspaper office and talked to Angus McCarren, Metro Editor of the Commercial Appeal, who called the FBI upon hearing their story. This initiated an investigation by the FBI of James Tague as the possible assassin of Martin Luther King. The file was closed in July 1968 with a handwritten notation at the bottom of the FBI memorandum "Northern is a nut." It had been almost 10 years after the assassination of Martin Luther King when I became aware that I had been investigated as his possible assassin.

HAROLD WEISBERG

One evening in the early 70's, I was home watching television when the phone rang. I answered and the man introduced himself as Harold Weisberg. He said he wanted to ask me some questions about the Kennedy assassination. I agreed and we talked at length about the assassination. Mr. Weisberg came across as very knowledgeable about the facts, and I was impressed with his knowledge about the events surrounding the assassination of President Kennedy. I did not realize it at the time, but some of the things that he told me were things that I had had a gut feeling about. Talking to Harold Weisberg that evening renewed my interest in the assassination. Some of the things he was telling me he was citing from the 26-volume report. When I got off the phone, I made up my mind to see if I could find a set of the 26 volumes that I could buy and see for myself what Harold had told me. I found a set and purchased it, and it was the start of 30 years of personal research on the assassination of John F. Kennedy and a great friendship with Harold Weisberg. Harold and I talked often and corresponded by mail frequently through the years. Whenever Harold discovered something new, he would share it with me and send me copies of what he had found. I never knew of anything that Harold told me that could not be backed up by documented evidence.

Harold Weisberg died February 21, 2002 at the age of 88 in Frederick, Maryland. Harold was often dubbed "the country's leading authority on the President John F. Kennedy and Martin Luther King assassinations," and those of us who have met and knew Harold agree. Harold had been a newspaper and magazine writer, a Senate investigator, and had been involved in intelligence analyses for a spy agency in World War II. His work was of great value to the Justice and Treasury Departments. During his life, Harold had been praised by correspondents, Congressmen, Cabinet members, and the

White House. In the late 30's, he worked for the chairman of the La Follette Civil Liberties Committee and had been consulted by other Congressional Committees, including The War Preparedness Committee, headed by then Senator Harry S. Truman. In the late 1940's, he turned to farm life with his wife Lillian and they won prizes for their poultry. They named their farm the "Coq d'or" farm. Harold and Lillian were early participants in the Peace Corps program and their "Geese for Peace" program, which shipped geese world-wide to be bred and raised in poverty-stricken countries, brought them international acclaim. Harold was also a gourmet cook, winning many prizes locally, and was named National Barbecue King in 1959.

In 1964 when the 26 volumes of the Warren Report became available to the public, Harold purchased the 26-volume report and poured over the testimony of witnesses and other evidence contained in the 26 volumes. Friends who knew him stated Harold had a photographic memory. When Harold found contradictions in eyewitness testimony and superficial research into the possibility of a conspiracy, he went to the F.B.I. for help in resolving these questions. Harold knew his way around Washington and expected the F.B.I.'s cooperation in resolving these issues by making available their files to him. Instead, Harold ran into a wall of secrecy erected by the F.B.I. and he was denied any help from them in resolving these issues. This turndown by the F.B.I. was the start of an obsession to find the truth about the Kennedy assassination and led to 35 years of financial hardship.

In 1965, Harold wrote his first book, one of the first books to raise questions about the Warren Report, WHITEWASH—THE REPORT ON THE WARREN REPORT. Once the book was finished, he went to publisher after publisher. The editors praised his book with remarks such as "a convincing document, impressive, certainly worthwhile, valid, reasoned and concerned, could be a best seller," but not one of these establishment publishers would publish the book. In 1965, you did not print something that could be considered critical of the Government or the F.B.I. Harold self-published the book and publicized it himself, selling over 30,000 copies. It was considered a literary success. Dell did then publish the book and a follow-up called WHITEWASH II: THE F.B.I.-SECRET SERVICE COVER UP in 1966. Other books were to follow, PHOTOGRAPHIC WHITEWASH, POST MORTEM, OSWALD IN NEW ORLEANS, CASE OF CONSPIRACY WITH THE C.I.A. (Canyon Books in 1967), MARTIN LUTHER KING THE ASSASSINATION (Carrol & Graf, 1993), and CASE OPEN: THE UNANSWERED JFK ASSASSINATION QUESTIONS (Carrol & Graf, 1994). There were also over 30 unpublished books that Harold wrote.

Harold Weisberg was the one person who brought suit against the United States Government under the Freedom of Information Act that led to the release of the F.B.I.'s Kennedy and King files. Harold had asked me to join him in these lawsuits, and I did. When the files were released by the F.B.I.,

Harold was one of the first to receive them. With the help of volunteer students from nearby Hood College, these files were organized into over 60 four-drawer filing cabinets in his basement. They remained there until he donated them to the Hood College Library late in his life. Harold also accumulated thousands of documents from other government agencies in his home and spent untold hours in the National Archives scouring millions more. Many researchers have spent many hours in Harold's basement, including myself.

I first came to know Harold when he called me one evening asking me questions about the missed shot that hit the curb in front of me. It was the start of a life-long friendship. I have been a guest in Harold and Lillian's home, and Harold has been a guest in my home in Dallas. Through the years, Harold was constantly going through the hundreds of thousands of pages of F.B.I. files in his basement, and when he would find something new and of unusual interest, he would send me a copy. On many occasions, Harold urged me to write the true story about the attempted cover up by the F.B.I. of a missed shot and my minor injury during the assassination of President Kennedy. Harold spent over 35 years, often seven days a week, in his quest for the truth in the assassination of President John F. Kennedy, and this dogged and unrelenting quest for the truth led him to conclude the possibility of a conspiracy or of a different assassin than Lee Harvey Oswald.

Through the years, Harold and I debated the many issues that had arisen since the release of the Warren Report, and one of those issues was that of a government cover-up of some sort. In my mind I had many unanswered questions about how the Warren Commission had come to some of the conclusions they had come to. I knew that F.B.I. Director J. Edgar Hoover's ego and uncooperative attitude had caused some of the problems, but that someone in our government would make a conscious effort to cover up the facts associated with the assassination of a President was something I had not accepted. I had suspicions of the possibility of a cover-up, but not the cold hard evidence to prove it. Harold had spent hours upon hours in the National Archives doing research on the assassination of President Kennedy, and in his research he had examined the scar on the curb section where a stray bullet had hit the street near where I was standing during the shooting. Over the years, Harold would tell me, "The hole in the curb has been patched." I would tell Harold that there never was a hole, " that only about an eighth of an inch was scrapped off the curb where the bullet had hit and ricocheted off the round of the curb." And Harold would reply back, "Well, it has been patched." After years of Harold telling me the hole in the curb had been patched and me explaining there never was a hole, I decided to just go examine the curb section myself in the National Archives and see what Harold was talking about.

THE BULLET MARK ON THE CURB

In April 1997, I made arrangements to fly to Washington D.C. to visit the National Archives. I wanted to view the piece of curbing that had been cut out of the street on August 5, 1964. A stray bullet had hit this piece of curb during the assassination of President John F. Kennedy on November 22, 1963. When I called the National Archives to see if I needed to make an appointment to view this curbing, I was told that the curb section was no longer available for viewing. With the help of my congressman's and one of my Senator's staffs, however, an appointment was made for me to view it. I armed myself with a high-powered magnifying glass and flew to Washington D.C. When I arrived at the National Archives at the appointed time, an assistant manager of the Archives led me to a room where the wooden crate containing the curb section had been set out for my inspection. When the assistant manager lifted the curb section out of the crate and placed it on the table, I did not need my magnifying glass; you could plainly see the place where the bullet had hit the curb. What had been a small gouge with some concrete dislodged was now smooth and of a different texture than the surrounding concrete. You could plainly see with the naked eye that someone had tampered with the curb where the bullet had hit. The half-inch by three-quarter-inch area where the bullet had hit was darker than the rest of the curb. A close examination of this area revealed that it had been patched by a mortar-like substance. Concrete has aggregate rock in it and mortar has sand in it. At the point of impact was mortar and the surrounding area was concrete. I remarked to the assistant manager, "It has been patched," and he replied, "Yes, it sure has, I can see that."

While at the Archives, I got clear copies of the photographs that F.B.I. Agent Shaneyfelt had taken of the curb just before it was cut from the street on August 5, 1964. The photograph labeled Shaneyfelt C.E. 30 reveals that the mark on the curb was still visible to the naked eye eight months after the assassination. It also reveals that the bullet mark had been patched sometime before it was cut out of the street in August 1964. When I left the Archives, my mind was full of questions as to why someone would patch this curb section with mortar. What was the importance of doing so? Why did the F.B.I. say at first they could not find the bullet mark on the curb? Here it was, just an ugly piece of cement, boxed in a wooden crate and stored in the National Archives. It was the physical proof that evidence in the assassination of President Kennedy had been tampered with.

As I drove my rental car to Frederick, Maryland to Harold Weisberg's house, I asked myself who, what, when, and why was the bullet mark patched? Harold knew about my appointment at the National Archives and was expecting me. He had laid out some papers for me on the table when I arrived, and when he handed the sheets of paper to me, he said you need to read this. The papers Harold handed to me were a letter addressed to a leading national magazine with an engineering report attached. The letter was dated March 17, 1983, with Reference: Examination of a portion of concrete curb kept at the National Archives, Washington D.C. The attached engineering report with the letter was from an Alexandria, Virginia engineering firm. The conclusion of the report was that the area where a bullet had hit the curb had been patched. There is no record that the magazine that had ordered the engineering report ever used the report in a story.

What Harold Weisberg had been telling me for years was true. The curb had been patched, but why? Harold and I had a long discussion about my involvement and the missed shot. We reviewed the history of this missed shot. We knew that the Warren Commission was preparing to wrap up its investigation in June 1964 when Jim Lehrer wrote the article in the DALLAS TIMES HERALD about a missed shot and me. We knew the missed curb shot had not been investigated, and I had not been called to testify before that article appeared. In fact there had been no investigation by the Warren Commission into the one shot that had completely missed the Presidential limousine and hit the curb near me sending debris into my face. Lehrer's story did stop the Warren Commission from concluding that the first shot hit the President, the second shot hit the Governor, and the third shot hit the President in the head. Their belated investigation of a shot that missed and hit the curb concluded that one shot did indeed go astray and hit the curb. It also forced the Commission to make a faulty conclusion, that one shot had hit both the President and the Governor.

Harold and I asked ourselves many questions. Up until the Lehrer article came out in June 1964, was the fact that one bullet had missed its target unknown? No, it was common knowledge. Witnesses had made statements in the Sheriff's office that very day about seeing the debris fly off the curb when a bullet hit the curb, and the Warren Commission had those statements. When a couple of these witnesses tried to say something about the bullet hitting the curb when they testified before the Warren Commission lawyers, they were sidetracked and ignored by the Commission staff lawyers taking their depositions. Deputy Sheriff Buddy Walthers was the first to find the scar on the curb and he had shown several fellow deputies the bullet mark on the curb that day. James Underwood and Tom Dillard had photographed the scar on the curb. The Sheriff's deputies and the photographers had all testified before the Warren Commission staff, before the Lehrer article appeared, but not one of them was asked about the scar on the curb, nor did they volunteer any information about a bullet hitting the curb. The statement I had given to the Dallas Police had disappeared into thin air, but the F.B.I. acknowledged they had the statement they took from me in my office on December 14, 1963. The F.B.I. and at least one person on the Warren Commission staff knew about a stray bullet hitting the curb long before June 1964. Why then was the scar on the curb patched, ignored, and some of the Commission lawyers acting like there was no missed shot? It is apparent, however, that J. Lee Rankin, Chief Counsel for the Warren Commission, did not know about a bullet hitting the curb. When Rankin became aware of the missed shot in June, he asked Hoover to have his F.B.I. agents find the place where the bullet had hit the curb. When Hoover reported back that they could not find any place where a bullet had hit, Rankin gave Hoover an ultimatum to find the mark. The F.B.I. located the mark on the curb in late July 1964.

Harold and I agreed that a bullet hitting the curb during the shooting was not a secret. So we tried to look at it in another way. Some of the questions we asked ourselves were: Why was I asked in the middle of my testimony why I was in Dealey Plaza in May 1964 taking movie pictures? Who knew I took those pictures? Was the F.B.I. tailing me in May for some reason? Why did the innocent film I took in Dealey Plaza disappear from my home? Why did the seven Warren Commission members, in their January meeting, question Hoover's adamant position about Oswald being the lone gunman, that there were three shots and all three shots hit in the limousine, and that there was no conspiracy? Why had the witnesses who saw the mark on the curb on November 22, 1963, not been asked about the missed shot or spoken up about the missed shot when they testified before the Warren Commission? Why were the witnesses who saw the debris fly from the curb when the bullet hit the curb ignored?

What happened to the statement that I gave at the Dallas Police station? Had the F.B.I. not given the statement I gave to them on December 14, 1963 to the Warren Commission? What reason was there for the curb section to be patched where a bullet had hit during the shooting? Why did the F.B.I. fight Harold Weisberg's Freedom of Information lawsuit for years over the spectrographic analysis of the curb and then finally state in the court room that this wafer thin film had been thrown away to make room for storage, and only doing so when it looked like the judge was going to rule in Weisberg's favor? What would this spectrographic analysis plate have revealed? Why did the F.B.I. at first say they could not find the mark where the bullet had hit the curb, and then suddenly find the mark the day after I testified before the Warren Commission? Why did the F.B.I. attempt to discredit me shortly after the Lehrer article? The attempted smear of my name did not work as the Warren Commission did not buy it. Harold and I wrestled with these questions and others. Everything pointed to the Federal Bureau of Investigation, but why the bother? Why was covering up this missed shot so important to the F.B.I.? Who else had the power and ability to control the outcome of the Warren Commission's investigation? There is a massive amount of evidence that there was an attempt to cover up that one shot went astray and hit the curb near me. Harold Weisberg and I could not come up with satisfactory answers to the aforementioned questions we asked of ourselves and these questions are part of why we will never know the full truth about the assassination of President Kennedy. We did ask ourselves one final question: Did J. Edgar Hoover fear that if it became public knowledge that one shot had missed, combined with all the other injuries to President Kennedy and Governor Connally, that it would prove that there was a conspiracy to kill President Kennedy, and that there were more than the three shots that were heard?

When it became known late in the investigation that there was a missed shot, the Warren Commission was forced to adopt the "magic bullet" theory, that one shot hit both men. That conclusion was erroneously based on a faulty artist drawing, however, that illustrated the President's back entry wound as being in the neck and above the throat "exit" wound, when in fact the actual entry wound was six inches lower than the artist illustration and below the throat "exit" wound.

In 1997, the curbing section that was removed from the street in Dallas on August 5, 1964 was in the National Archives in a patched condition, and if it is still there and in the same condition as it was then, it is proof positive that evidence concerning the assassination of President Kennedy was tampered with.

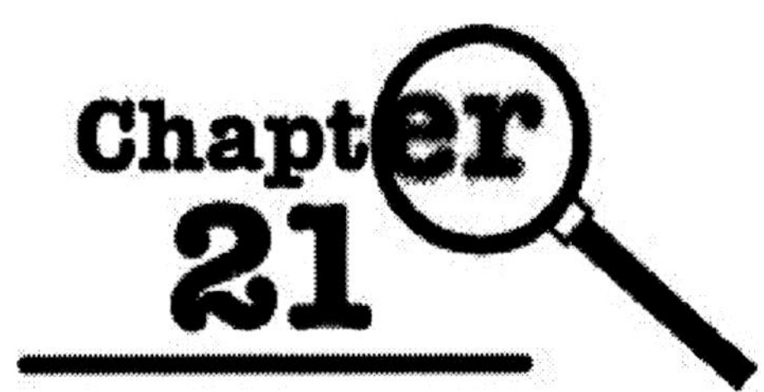

NO COPPER WAS FOUND

When the curb section containing the spot where a bullet had hit during the shooting was finally removed from the street on August 5, 1964, it was sent to the F.B.I. laboratory for testing. The laboratory performed a spectrographic analysis on the now altered and patched mark where a bullet had hit on November 22, 1963.

On August 12, 1964, F.B.I. Director J. Edgar Hoover sent a letter to J. Lee Rankin, Chief Counsel for the Warren Commission, about the lab report on the spectrographic analysis of the curb. Hoover stated that the lab report showed that lead and traces of antimony were found at the point of impact on the curb, but no trace of copper was found. Part of Hoover's letter reads thus: "The absence of copper precludes the possibility that the mark on the curbing section was made by an un-mutilated military-type full-jacketed bullet such as the bullet from Governor Connally's stretcher, C1, or the bullet or bullets represented by the jacket fragments, C2 and C3, found in the presidential limousine. Further, the damage to the curbing would have been much more extensive if a rifle bullet had struck the curbing without first having struck some other object. Therefore, this mark could not have been made by the first impact of a high velocity rifle bullet." To the Warren Commission's credit, it dismissed the implications of Hoover's letter and found that one shot did in fact go wild and hit the curb. Hoover's remark in his letter to Rankin about more extensive damage to the curb if it had not struck something else first caught my attention when I read his remarks in 1964. I asked myself at that time where Hoover was coming from. I saw the damage, I felt the damage that day, and I did so within minutes of the assassination. There was very noticeable damage to the curb, but I let it go. This was our esteemed F.B.I. and they knew what they were doing. What I did not know in 1964 was that the damage to the curb had been patched with a mortar like substance before the curb had been cut out of the street on August 5, 1964 and sent to the F.B.I. lab for analyses. A close study of available photographs taken that day shows that from where I was standing and the way Elm Street curves, the President's limousine was heading directly toward me and head on when the fatal headshot occurred. For a bullet to have hit something or someone in the President's limousine and a fragment from that bullet to fly out of the limousine with enough velocity to hit the curb with enough force to dislodge cement from the round of the curb, the fragment would have had to have penetrated the windshield of the limousine and there was no hole in the windshield. There was a crack on the inside of the windshield, but no hole. Also, the laws of physics tell us that if a fragment had looped up in the air and over the windshield, it would have already lost its energy and just plopped at my feet. The bullet did not hit the curb head on, it hit at an angle and left a half-inch wide mark three quarters of an inch long at the round of the curb where the side of the curb rounds onto the top of the curb. There was no way for this bullet to dig into the curb and expend its energy; it could only ricochet off the cement.

That Hoover reported to the Warren Commission that there was an absence of copper at the point of impact on the curb was disturbing to me. I knew in my own mind that it was not a fragment, but that a whole bullet had hit the curb and left a half-inch wide scar. The official Warren Report agreed with me that it was a whole bullet, not a fragment, and that one shot did miss and hit the curb in front of me. The F.B.I. lab report still disturbed me though. Then I found in volume XX, page 2, of the 26-volume Warren Report a letter from J. Edgar Hoover to J. Lee Rankin about another spectrographic analysis that had no trace of copper. No trace of copper was found in the President's shirt or tie where a bullet had penetrated those articles of clothing. It is interesting to note that J. Edgar Hoover did not make the same point about the shirt and tie spectrographic analyses that he did about the curb analysis, that the shirt and tie analysis showed no trace of copper, and if there was no trace of copper found, that it had to be a fragment that penetrated the shirt and tie, since no copper was found. So why did Hoover make an issue about the curb point of impact not showing a trace of copper, when there were at least two other spectrographic analyses that said there were no traces of copper in some of the President's clothing that was supposed to have been penetrated by an intact bullet and not a fragment of a bullet? These two letters, written at different times, both mentioning no trace of copper, raised a host of questions. Among them was the question whether there was a second gunman using a different type of ammunition than the pristine copper-jacketed bullet found at Parkland Hospital. The bigger question, however, was why did the F.B.I. fight Harold Weisberg in court for years against releasing the spectrographic analysis plate for an outside expert opinion on what the analysis would reveal? If the F.B.I. spectrograph analysis showed no trace of copper and was correct, an outside expert opinion would verify that there was no trace of copper and no harm would be done.

Harold Weisberg was one of the first to question the Warren Commission findings and sought the help of the F.B.I. and its files to assist in resolving some of the questions that had arisen. He was flat turned down for any help from the F.B.I. We now know that J. Edgar Hoover had given instructions to the F.B.I. employees and agents not to cooperate with Harold in any way. Harold did not give up easily though and he brought several lawsuits against the U.S. Government under the Freedom of Information Act for release of information. One of those lawsuits was for the release of the wafer thin plate that was used for the spectrographic analysis of the curb. Harold wanted an independent and separate examination of the spectrographic plate by an independent agency. That the F.B.I. analysis stated there was no trace of copper had serious implications about the number of shots and the possibility that another weapon with different bullets might have been used in the assassination. Harold's lawsuit dragged on for years with the F.B.I. lawyers vigorously fighting the release of this spectrographic plate. The lawsuit ended when in the Federal Courtroom the F.B.I. lawyers announced that the wafer thin spectrograph plate had been lost or thrown away to make room for storage.

JACK RUBY
THE MURDER OF LEE HARVEY OSWALD

Jack Ruby shot and killed Lee Harvey Oswald in the Dallas Police Headquarters basement less than 48 hours after the assassination of President John F. Kennedy. Ruby's killing of Oswald occurred in front of millions of television viewers. The Dallas Police Department was in the process of transferring accused Presidential assassin Oswald to the Dallas County jail when Oswald was shot and killed by Ruby. Over the weekend, there had been threats on Oswald's life. The Dallas Police had received several crank calls, and there were rumors about vigilantes taking action. When Dallas Police Chief Jesse Curry arrived in his office that morning, he was told regarding one of the calls "about 100 men are going to take the prisoner Oswald and we do not want any policemen hurt." The Dallas Police made what they thought were intensive security plans to insure a safe transfer of Oswald to the Dallas County jail. Oswald's time of transfer was unannounced to the public or the Press. The basement was searched, officers were posted to guard all entrances, an armored truck decoy was put in place, and only accredited, known reporters were allowed into the basement.

Oswald had been arrested in the Oak Cliff section of Dallas as a suspect in the killing of a Dallas Police officer shortly after the assassination of the President. It was quickly discovered by Dallas Police that Oswald was an employee of the Texas Schoolbook Depository, the building in which it was suspected that the shots were fired that killed the President and injured Texas Governor John Connally. Oswald was quickly charged with both murders, and in less than 48 hours, the press had tried and convicted Oswald. On that Sunday morning, November 24, 1963, less than 48 hours after the assassination of President Kennedy on November 22, 1963, Oswald was a hated man, already convicted by the Dallas police, the F.B.I., and the press for the assassination of President Kennedy, the wounding of Texas Governor John Connally, and the killing of a Dallas Policeman. The one and only topic of conversation that weekend was the assassination of our President and Lee Harvey Oswald. In those conversations statements were often made such as "they ought to just take Oswald and string him up."

Jack Rubenstein, better known as Jack Ruby, was a struggling strip club owner and a small-time hustler. He knew underworld characters, had some mob connections, and often sought favor and friendship with members of the Dallas Police Department. Jack Ruby almost always carried a gun. Texas law allowed a businessman to carry a gun when taking cash receipts to the bank. This law was not strictly enforced when a businessman carried a gun at other times. Although Ruby was known to have a quick temper, he was not considered a dangerous man and he was likeable. I had met Jack Ruby on a couple of occasions. The first time was at his sister's dance hall in the Oak Lawn area, where Ruby was going from table to table, introducing himself, handing out business cards, promoting his Carousel Club and giving out free passes to the club. I did use my free pass to his strip club and what I remember most about the visit to his club was his comedian, Wally Weston, who was very funny. When the strippers in Ruby's club were through stripping, they still had almost as much on as some of the women we see today on prime-time television.

Jim Levelle was the Dallas Police Homicide officer with the white hat, who was handcuffed to Lee Harvey Oswald when Jack Ruby shot and killed Oswald in the basement of the Dallas Police Station two days after the assassination of President Kennedy. Jim Levelle had known Jack Ruby for many years. In an interview with Jim Levelle at his Garland, Texas home, Jim confirmed something to me that I had felt sure of for many years, that Jack Rubenstein was not a part of any plot. It was pure happenstance that Ruby was there at that exact moment to shoot Oswald. In Jim Levelle's words: "From Friday night on, we had numerous threats that they were going to take Oswald away from us and do all sorts of bodily damage to him. Even when it came out we were going to transfer him in an armored vehicle, there were some messages that came in that they were going to barricade the street and turn the armored vehicle over and set it on fire. All of this was going through my mind at the time we were coming down the elevator to the basement in the police station with Oswald to transport him to the Dallas County jail. If it, Ruby shooting Oswald, had happened outside on the street, I would not have thought too much about it, because I was expecting an attempt on his life. But for it to happen in the basement was a total shock to me and as I have pointed out a lot of times, as you can see the expression on my face you know that it was a shock, as I walked out into the basement from the police elevator and they turned on all of those floodlights for the cameras. Momentarily I was blinded. But they had told me the car to transport Oswald to the county jail would be crossways of the entrance, so that all I would have to do was walk right into the back door of the squad car, however it was not there because of the crowd of news people that had gathered and detective Charles Daugherty who was driving the car that we were going to use had parked the car in a different position. I might add and I will explain a little later, we had had to abandon the armored vehicle that we were going to use because we could not get it into the basement, because of the air conditioning system on its roof. It would not go under the entrance, so we had to revert back to the car as we originally wanted to use anyway. As I walked out I was looking to my right to see where the car was and out of the corner of my eye I saw Ruby standing there right in the center of the driveway. He had his pistol by his side and then he took two quick steps and double-actioned into the midriff of Oswald and shot Oswald. Later, I and Bill Alexander, the Assistant D.A., timed that sequence with the cameras and it took just a little over one second, about a second and a half for Ruby to take that step, those two short steps and double-actioned, like one thousand and one is about how much time it took him to make those short steps, so I was not able to react, to prevent him from shooting Oswald. I did, since I had my hand held in his belt, jerk back on Oswald, trying to pull him behind me. But all I did was turn his body so that instead of the bullet hitting him dead center it hit him about 4 inches to the left of his navel. The bullet went all the way through Oswald and lodged just under the skin on the other side. If he had had better ammunition the bullet would have gone on through and hit me roughly in the middle of my left side. When I later picked Oswald up along with Officer Combest and carried him back into the jail hall and laid him down, Officer Combest took my handcuffs off of Oswald. I examined Oswald and could see and feel the bullet under his skin, you could roll it around, it was on his right side just under the rib cage. It was just the thickness of his skin from going on through Oswald's body. Many times people have said how close did you come from getting shot and I said just the thickness of the skin because if it had gone through him it would have hit me in the left side. The ambulance was there in about three minutes and we loaded him into the ambulance and I rode with him to Parkland. In the Trauma Room at Parkland the Doctor pinched the bullet and hit the skin with a scapel and the bullet popped out into a little silver tray. I had the nurse scratch her initial on the end of the bullet while I watched. The official time of death at the hospital was 1:07 P.M.; but my opinion is that half way to the hospital Oswald stretched and groaned and went completely limp and I always thought that was when he probably expired. I was holding his pulse and I could not find a pulse. Oswald lapsed into unconsciousness almost immediately after being shot and was unconscious when he hit the floor. After we carried Oswald back to the hall floor, I tried to say something to him but his eyes were closed and he never responded. I transferred Jack Ruby on Monday morning to the County jail and on the way there I asked him why he shot Oswald. He told me "I just wanted to be a hero but it looks like I just fouled things up good". Later on I got to thinking about 13 years earlier when I was new on the department working in uniform patrol, one of the things we did in the evening was go through the night clubs and dance halls and see if there was anybody in there getting drunk that might create a disturbance when the place closed, if so, we would just ease them out. It was very seldom that we would have to put anybody in jail. They would leave when we told them that we thought they had too much to drink. On one of those occasions when we were checking the Silver Spur that Ruby owned in 1950, located on South Ervay Street here in Dallas, I was talking with Ruby while my partner circulated through the dance hall to see if anybody in there was getting out of hand. Ruby told me that he had had a dream of finding two police officers in a death struggle about to lose their life, so that he could jump in there and save them and be a hero. Through the years I have felt that was Jack Ruby's only thought when he decided to kill Oswald. That he would be a hero and people from all over the world would come to the Carousel Club to shake the hand of the man who killed the assassin that killed President Kennedy.

"Several years later I (Jim Levelle) made this same statement to some television people and it went out on the air. A retired federal agent who had heard what I had said about Ruby on the air, called me and said, 'Jim, you do not know me' and asked me where I had come up with this idea about Ruby wanting to be a hero. I replied just from knowledge of knowing Jack Ruby, that I did not get it from anybody. The agent said it would be interesting to note that he was the F.B.I. agent assigned to interview all of Ruby's employees after the assassination and that is exactly the same picture that all of Jack Ruby's employees painted of Ruby. Jack Ruby thought he would be hero for killing Lee Harvey Oswald."

It is important to know that there was no announced or set time to transfer Lee Harvey Oswald to the Dallas County jail on that Sunday morning, November 24, 1963. Before being transferred, Oswald was to undergo some last minute interrogation by local, state, and Federal authorities and there was no time limit put on how long that interrogation would take. While Oswald was being interrogated, Jack Ruby received a call at his apartment from Teresa Norton, one of his strippers who lived in Fort Worth, asking for money. Jack Ruby agreed he would send Ms. Norton some money and went to the Western Union office down the street from the Dallas Police station and wired $25 to Teresa Norton in Fort Worth. The receipt for this Western Union wire was in Ruby's possession when he was arrested.

It was stamped by Western Union at 11:17 A.M., and the killing of Oswald occurred at 11:21 A.M. That was four minutes between the time the receipt was stamped at Western Union and the shooting of Oswald. A couple of weeks after the assassination, Jim Levelle went to the Western Union office and interviewed the clerk who was on duty that morning. The clerk explained his procedure was to stamp the receipt at the moment he was paid for the wire. Jim Levelle then walked off the route from Western Union office to the entrance to the basement of the police station three times and timed himself, once at a fast pace, once at a slow pace, and once at a normal pace. The average time to walk from the Western Union Office to the top of the ramp that led to the police basement was two minutes and twenty seconds, but add on a few seconds to walk down the ramp. That left just a little over a minute unaccounted for. The Dallas Police had not announced the time that they would be transferring Oswald to the Dallas County jail and had in fact not set an exact time for themselves to do the transfer. They did initially plan to transfer Oswald earlier that morning, but a last minute interrogation of Oswald took longer than expected. If the questioning of Oswald that morning had not taken so long, Oswald would have already been transferred to the Dallas County jail when Ruby arrived at the Police Station.

As for Ruby getting into the basement, it was too simple, and I will again quote Jim Levelle as to what Ruby had told him. "I (Ruby) knew that I could not get into the basement but thought I would walk over to the entrance ramp to the basement of the police station and look down the ramp and see what I could see." But as fate would have it, just as Jack Ruby was about to walk up to the ramp to the basement, Lt. Reo Pierce came up the ramp in a squad car. Officer Roy Vaughn, who had been assigned to guard the ramp, saw Lt. Pierce coming up the ramp and stepped out into the street to hold up traffic on Main Street so Lt. Pierce could make a left turn across oncoming traffic. The altered plan was for Lt. Pierce to lead the armored car as a decoy to the real transfer. As Lt. Pierce was turning onto Main Street, with Officer Roy Vaughn holding up traffic for Lt. Pierce to make a left turn, Officer Vaughn's back was turned to the ramp. It was at this very moment that Jack Ruby arrived at the ramp from the Western Union office and walked casually and unobstructed down the ramp into the basement of the police station.

There can be only one conclusion. Ruby's shooting of Oswald was not planned, was not a part of any sinister plot to silence Oswald. That Jack Ruby was at the Western Union Telegraph office in downtown Dallas to send a wire to an employee was not planned. Jack Ruby got into the basement by accident because a Dallas Policeman momentarily walked out onto the street and stopped traffic for a superior officer to exit the basement of the Police Station onto the street. Due to an eerie set of unplanned timing and circumstances, Ruby just happened to be at the right place at the right time to kill Oswald. Ruby always carried a gun, and with Oswald being ushered out into the basement right in front of him, Ruby made a split second decision that he would be a hero if he killed Oswald.

What we did not know for years after the assassination, and only after a long court battle using the Freedom of Information Act to force the F.B.I. to release their files on the assassination of President Kennedy, was that Jack Ruby was a paid F.B.I. informant at the time he murdered Lee Harvey Oswald in front of millions of television viewers. In murdering Oswald, Ruby had acted on a split second impulse that had absolutely nothing to do with the F.B.I. F.B.I. Director J. Edgar Hoover knew, however, that if it got out that Ruby was on the F.B.I.'s payroll as an informant when he killed Oswald, the F.B.I.'s prestigious public image that had taken years for Hoover to nurture and build would be seriously questioned, damaged, or even ruined by public outrage if it became public knowledge. Hoover knew that it did not matter that Ruby had acted alone and on his own; the mere fact that Ruby was on the F.B.I. payroll as an informant was enough to bring suspicion upon the F.B.I. This writer believes that this revelation regarding Ruby killing Oswald, along with other facts, was the driving force behind Hoover's haste to wrap up the case. Oswald was the man; close the case. Jack Ruby died of cancer in a Dallas County jail cell.

THE SHOT THAT HIT THE PRESIDENT IN THE BACK

THE FIRST SHOT

The Warren Commission concluded that it was probably the first shot that hit the President in the back and also caused all of Governor Connally's injuries. The Commission also concluded that this first shot hit the President in the neck near the collar line and exited the President's throat. According to their report, after exiting the President's throat, the bullet then hit Governor Connally in the back near his right armpit and shattered a rib, exiting his chest near the right nipple. The bullet then hit the back of the Governor's right wrist and shattered the wrist. The bullet then exited the palm side of the wrist and penetrated about three inches into the thigh and deposited a fragment in the thighbone or femur. The Warren Commission concluded that this bullet then worked its way out of the Governor's thigh and was found on the floor after rolling off of a stretcher that had been placed outside the emergency room at Parkland Hospital. The bullet that was found on the floor at Parkland Hospital was in pristine condition. That one bullet had caused all these injuries and was still in pristine condition raised questions. When the Warren Commission's 26-volume report was released to the public in late 1964, the Commission's own evidence contained in these 26 volumes contradicted the conclusion that one bullet had penetrated the bodies of both men. In fact, the conclusion that one bullet penetrated both men's bodies caused doubt about the truthfulness of the entire Warren Report. The critics soon named this pristine bullet, Commission Exhibit 399, the "magic bullet." It did not take a team of criminologists to determine that this was a false conclusion, that one bullet hit both men. The

Commission's own published evidence, with details of the reenactment of the shooting, prove that it was impossible for one bullet to injure both men. Through the years critics blamed the Warren Commission for deliberately misleading the public for the conclusion that this "magic bullet" hit both men. When one studies all the evidence, they will find that a key piece of evidence that the Warren Commission staff relied on to reach its conclusions was faulty.

The seven members of the Warren Commission relied heavily on the 14 Warren Commission staff lawyers for finding all the basic facts involved in the assassination of President Kennedy. When these seven Commission members were presented with the conclusions of their staff, there was disagreement among the seven members about those conclusions. The validity of the single bullet theory, that one bullet hit both men, was at the center of one of those disagreements. Three of the Commission members, Senator Richard Russell, Senator John Cooper, and Representative Hale Boggs believed that there might have been separate bullets. Representative Boggs had mild doubts, but Senator Russell and Senator Cooper refused to accept the single bullet theory. These three members wanted to wait three or four months to gather more evidence, but there was tremendous pressure from the press and the White House to get the final report out. In a September 18, 1964 Commission meeting, a compromise was reached among the seven members that the solution to presenting the evidence of a single bullet causing injuries to both men was to use the word "persuasive" in the final report.

The Abraham Zapruder amateur movie shows that President Kennedy is reacting to already being hit in the back as he emerges from behind a sign in frame 225. In this frame, the President is starting to raise his hands and arms as if he had been surprised by a punch in the back. This frame shows Mrs. Kennedy also reacting to the shot and reaching for her husband. For the President to be reacting to being hit in frame 225, he had to have been hit by frame 215 or earlier. The most probable evidence is that the President was hit between frames 210 and 212. In the reenactment of the shooting by the Warren Commission, at frame 210 the President's limousine is 139 feet from the corner of Houston and Elm streets, 177 feet from the sixth floor window, and 349 feet from the triple underpass. At frame 210, the angle of the shot from the sixth floor of the Schoolbook Depository would be 21.34 degrees. In the reenactment, using a telescope mounted on a rifle from the sixth floor window and aiming down at the rear collar line of the President, the bullet could possibly have exited the President's throat, but the downward trajectory of the bullet would have then entered Governor Connally's body lower than the Governor's actual wound. The undisputed facts reveal that the bullet that hit President Kennedy in the back, actually <u>hit the President five and one half inches below the</u>

collar line near the third thoracic vertabra, and not in the neck near the collar line. The problem that caused this erroneous conclusion by the Warren Commission was that the autopsy photos were not available to the Warren Commission. The Commission and its staff had to rely on an artist drawing made two days after the autopsy by an artist who was not at the autopsy and had also not viewed any of the autopsy photos. The artist drawing wrongly placed the President's back wound near the collar line in the neck/shoulder area. Dr. Humes' original autopsy face sheet does place the President's back wound about six inches below the collar and in the back. President Kennedy's personal physician signed and confirmed the original autopsy face sheet. Four other medical professionals who attended the autopsy confirmed the location of the back injury as being about six inches below the collar. The most solid evidence, and it still exists today, is that there are bullet holes in the President's coat and shirt five and three quarter inches below the collar line in the back. When you apply these undisputed facts, that this bullet hit the President nearly six inches below the collar and in the back at a downward angle of 21 degrees, the bullets downward energy, after hitting him in the back six inches below the collar at a 21 degree downward angle, would have propelled the bullet into the President's chest cavity and that the point of entry into the back was well below the throat wound. Further, with this bullet's trajectory, if it had penetrated and exited the President, it would have hit Governor Connally in the buttocks or lower and would have had to penetrate the back of the Governor's jump seat before hitting the Governor.

The position of Governor Connally in the Presidential limousine also debunks the theory that one shot hit both men. Photos taken in Dealey Plaza during the shooting reveal that the Governor was sitting in the far right position in the limousine. Assuming that the shot that hit the President in the back did exit his throat and did come from the sixth floor window of the Schoolbook Depository, it would mean that the shot came from the right rear of the limousine and was moving in a right to left trajectory. The President was hit slightly to the right of the spinal column at a right to left angle and was sitting behind the Governor slightly to the Governor's left. For the Governor to have also been hit by this bullet, the bullet would, after exiting the President's body, had to have somehow in mid-air jumped back to its right, then have made an abrupt left downward turn to have hit the Governor in the chest near his right armpit. A bullet traveling at 2,000 feet per second cannot do that. Governor Connally was hit by a separate bullet, just as the Governor stated he was hit by a separate bullet when he testified before the Warren Commission.

A notation in the autopsy report that the autopsy doctors could only probe the President's back wound an inch further complicated the issues of the first shot and the President's back wound. To my knowledge there is no discussion, explanation, or follow up in the Warren Report as to why the autopsy doctors could not trace this bullet's path through the President's body. Through the years I have had a nagging thought about the inability of the autopsy doctors to probe this wound and trace the bullet's path. I will share that thought with you. I and almost every other witness in Dealey Plaza that day described the first shot as sounding like the pop of a firecracker or an engine backfire. Even in the President's limousine, a Secret Service agent in the front seat described the first shot as sounding like the pop of a firecracker. Mrs. Kennedy, riding beside the President, described it as sounding like a motorcycle backfire. The first shot that I and other witnesses heard did not have the "crack" of a rifle shot as did the second and third shots. The bullet found on the floor at Parkland Hospital was in pristine condition and it was never determined from which stretcher it fell, the President's or the Governor's. It was assumed by the Warren Commission staff that it fell from Governor Connally's stretcher. My nagging thoughts have been, was the first shot a dud? Did it only penetrate the President's body an inch? Did this bullet then work its way out of the President's back as the Parkland Doctors worked on the President? Was the pristine bullet found on the floor at Parkland Hospital actually a dud that sounded like the pop of a firecracker when it was fired and only penetrated the President's body an inch? (See opposite page.)

Then there is the President's throat wound, which the Parkland doctors and nurses described as an entrance wound. The autopsy doctors completely missed this wound while doing the autopsy and it was not until the next day that the chief autopsy doctor, Dr. Humes, learned of this wound while talking to one of the attending physicians at Parkland Hospital and added it to the autopsy report as an after thought. It is easy to see why three of the seven members of the Warren Commission wanted another three or four months of investigation to determine more of the facts.

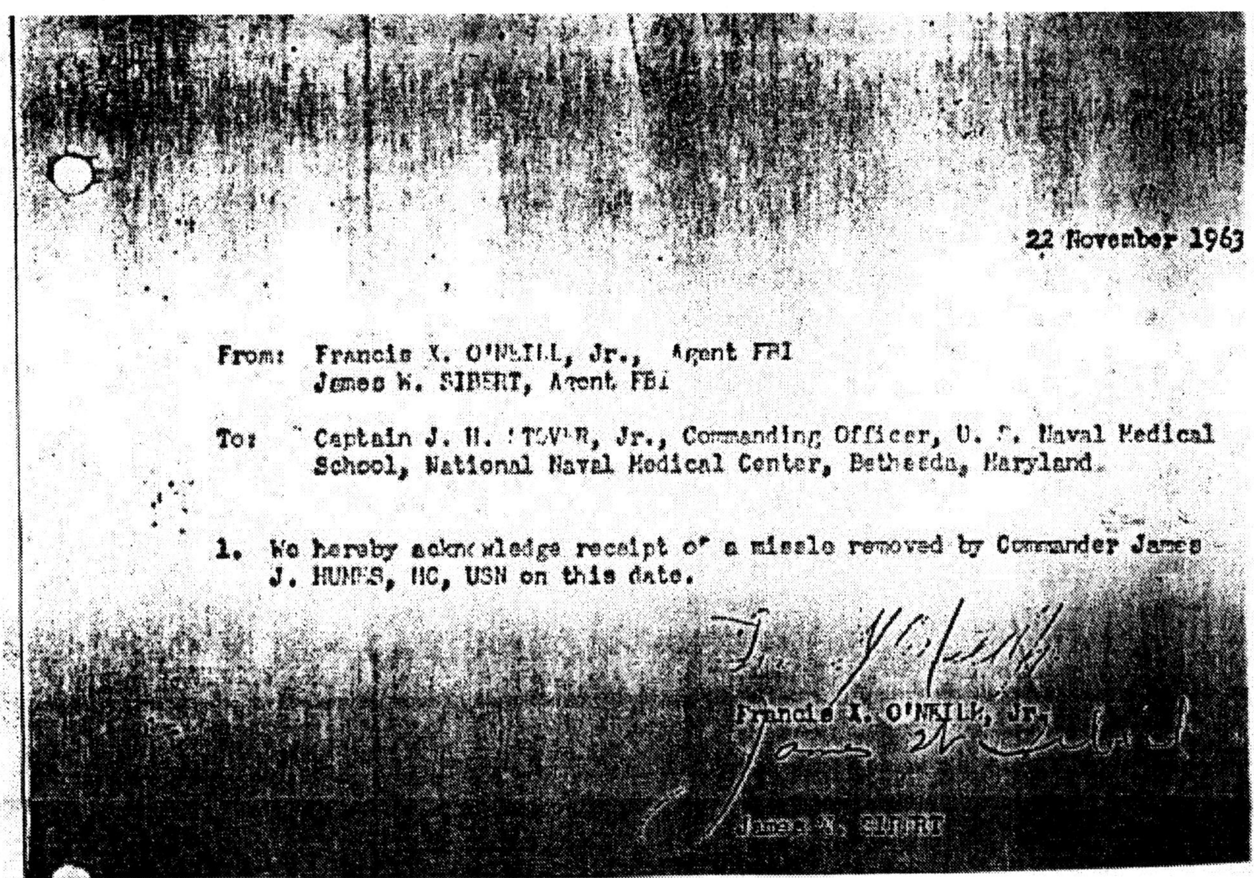

22 November 1963

From: Francis X. O'NEILL, Jr., Agent FBI
James W. SIBERT, Agent FBI

To: Captain J. H. STOVER, Jr., Commanding Officer, U. S. Naval Medical School, National Naval Medical Center, Bethesda, Maryland.

1. We hereby acknowledge receipt of a missle removed by Commander James J. HUMES, MC, USN on this date.

Francis X. O'NEILL, Jr.

James W. SIBERT

This is a copy of the receipt for a bullet removed from President Kenendy's body by Dr. James J. Humes during the President's autopsy the evening of November 22, 1963. It was given to F.B.I. agents Francis X. O'Neill, Jr. and James W. Sibert by Naval Captain J. W. Stovar, Commanindg Officer, U.S. Naval Medical School, National Medical Center, Bethesda, Maryland, who was in attendance at the autopsy.

This receipt was found among the thousands of documents the F.B.I. was forced to turn over under the Freedom of Information Act concerning the assassination of President John F. Kennedy. Admiral Calvin Galloway, also in attendance at the autopsy, confirmed that the missile was a whole bullet and not a missile fragment. This bullet never surfaced again in the investigation of the President's assassination, and the members of the Warren Commission and its staff were unaware that there had in fact been a whole bullet removed from the President's body during the autopsy.

Although the word missile is misspelled as "missle," this receipt for a bullet is critical to the fact that the evidence concerning the President's assassination was tampered with and proves without any doubt that there was a minimum of four shots fired during the assassination.

THE SHOT THAT HIT THE PRESIDENT IN THE HEAD

THE SECOND SHOT

The second shot hit the President in the head, blowing brain tissue, blood, and skull fragments in all directions. The Warren Commission's findings on this shot were just as controversial, if not more so, as their findings on the first shot. The Warren Commission determined this shot hit the back of the President's head and came from the sixth floor window. The Zapruder amateur movie captured the President's head exploding on film. The fatal headshot came at frame 313 in the Zapruder movie, and this frame is clear and graphic. According to the F.B.I. reenactment of the shooting, the President was 231 feet from the west curb of Houston Street, 265 feet from the sixth floor window, and 260 feet from the triple underpass. The angle of the rifle shooting down on the President was 15.21 degrees. The President's limousine was directly in front of Abraham Zapruder when this shot occurred. A copy of this frame can be found in volume XVIII, page 94 of the 26-volume report.

All evidence clearly indicates that there was a shot from the rear that hit the President in the back of the head. The autopsy doctors found a bullet hole in the rear upper part of the President's head and over 40 minute bullet fragments in the frontal part of his head indicating a shot from the rear. There was a crack on the inside of the windshield of the limousine. A piece of chrome molding over the windshield had a large dent in the molding.

What the Warren Commission omitted from their report was frames 314, 315, and 316. These frames show the head being snapped back so violently after being hit by a bullet that the momentum of the head movement slams the President's body and shoulders into the back of the seat. The Warren

Commission did not address the contradiction that the impact of a bullet would cause the object that was hit to react toward where the bullet came from in such a violent way. Through the years, I have asked scores of hunters if they have ever seen an animal they had fatally shot react toward them. Not one hunter could even imagine such a reaction; they all said that the impact of a bullet blows the object away from the source of the shot. The best witnesses were the railroad men who had gathered on top of the triple underpass to watch the Presidential motorcade. They had a panoramic view of Dealey Plaza. Two of those railroad men testified that they saw a puff of smoke during the shooting arise from behind the grassy knoll near the trees and picket fence. A couple more of the railroad men who were not called to testify made separate statements that they saw that puff of smoke. Being a man who had grown up with a rifle in my hand, I had never seen a puff of smoke come from a rifle barrel when it was fired and I did not give much weight to the "puff of smoke" testimony. Much later, I did speak to one firearms expert who told me a well-oiled barrel would cause a puff of smoke to come out of the barrel when the rifle was fired. Then one evening I was watching the gulf war news on television and they were showing Saddam Hussein, the President of Iraq. In the news clip Hussein had a rifle in his hand, pointed the rifle in the air, and fired it; a large puff of smoke came out of the barrel.

The Warren Commission, for the most part, ignored the possibility that the President could have also been hit in the head from the front at the same time he was hit in the head from behind. There is strong evidence that the President was indeed hit from the front as well as in back of the head. The attending Parkland physicians, almost to a man, stated the back of the President's head had been blown out. When Malcomb Killduff, assistant White House Press Secretary, announced to the world at Parkland that the President was dead, he pointed to his right temple as the point of entry of the fatal shot. When the House Assassinations Committee reopened the investigation in the late 70's, they determined that there was a simultaneous shot that hit the President from the front, but the pro-Warren Report backers clouded that conclusion. To admit that there was more than one shooter would mean that there was a conspiracy to kill the President.

The Warren Commission left open whether it was the second or third shot that hit the President in the head, but leaned heavily toward the headshot being the third shot and the second shot being the missed shot. In using the third shot, the Commission had to jam three shots into a five and one half second time span. It was determined that the Zapruder camera filmed 18.3 frames per second and at that speed it would be the time between frames 212 the first shot, and 313 the headshot. The Warren Commission had experts try to duplicate three shots in five and one half seconds with the same type of rifle and they could not. No one has ever duplicated what they say the shooter did that day.

What the Warren Commission overlooked and/or ignored were the Dealey Plaza witnesses who heard the shots that day and what they had to say about the time interval between the first and second shots. With few exceptions, witness after witness noted a noticeable delay between the first and second shots. I was one of those witnesses. What I heard that day in Dealey Plaza was that the first shot sounded like a firecracker going off and then thinking what kind of fool would light a firecracker with the President going by, that the police were going to grab him and he was in deep trouble. My thought process at that very moment was logical, not rushed, not excited, and I further remember with these thoughts in my mind that I tried to see into the crowd in front of the Schoolbook Depository whether that was the source of the firecracker, and what was going on there. As I was peering into the crowd to see what was going on, there was the crack of a high-powered rifle shot. By timing myself through these same thoughts that I had at that moment up until I heard the crack of a rifle shot, it took five to six seconds to repeat these same thoughts in repeated timings. There is no evidence in any of the 26 volumes of the Warren Report that any witness was questioned about the time between the first and second shots. If the Warren Commission had pursued questioning the Dealey Plaza witnesses about the interval between the first and second shots, they would have determined that there were indeed five to six seconds between the first and second shots. It would also explain that the shooter had time, five or six seconds, to work the bolt and inject another bullet into the rifle chamber, aim, and get off an accurate shot with ease.

THE SHOT THAT MISSED
THE THIRD SHOT

For years, when someone would ask me which shot missed, I would reply, "I do not know which shot missed. I just know it was not the first shot that missed and hit the curb near me." Gerald Posner broke me from making that statement. In his book CASE CLOSED, he quotes me as saying, "I do not know which shot missed," and he conveniently omits "I just know it was not the first shot that missed and hit the curb near me." I do not recall ever talking to Gerald Posner, but it is possible that I did. I still to this day, almost forty years after the assassination of President Kennedy, get calls from people asking me questions. Posner might have been one of those people. That Posner bases his book on the first shot missing the President is a fantasy.

From where I was standing I heard the pop of a firecracker and the crack of two rifle shots, no echoes, and only a slight reverberation from the second and third gunshots. That I only heard three shots has left me puzzled to this day, and I have never been able to account to myself for all the things that only three shots did that day. But I will cover that in another chapter. One thing that I have always been positive of is that the first shot was not the shot that hit the curb near me. It must be noted that the first shot did not have the sound of a rifle shot, the crack of a rifle shot that anyone familiar with gunfire knows. It was the sound of a firecracker going off. Most witnesses who were in Dealey Plaza that day and gave statements noted the same thing. The first shot sounded like a firecracker. When I testified before the Warren Commission, I testified that it was either the second or third shot that missed, and if I had to make a guess, it was the second shot that missed. Today with the advantage of time to thoroughly study the testimony of other witnesses and compare to my firsthand knowledge, I can now safely say and with confidence that it was the third shot that missed. When the first shot that sounded like a "firecracker" went off, my mind was fully focused, clear, and thinking who is that idiot setting off fireworks with the President going by. The second and third shots were not that clear. Now, by carefully studying the Zapruder movie and other witness testimonies, the first and second shots can be totally eliminated as the shot that missed. With my own eyewitness knowledge, and by comparing the statements of other eyewitnesses to the facts I am personally aware of, I can state with authority and without hesitation that it was the third shot that missed. There were many witnesses who saw the debris fly up when the third shot hit the curb. I have been able to identify at least 12 credible witnesses who testified before the Warren Commission or gave separate statements that they saw the bullet hit the curb. I am sure that there were many more witnesses who saw the bullet hit the curb and who never testified. Again, from a careful study of these known witness testimonies and statements, along with my personal knowledge, there can be only one conclusion. It was the third shot that went wild and hit the curb near where I was standing.

Stavis Ellis was a long-time veteran of the Dallas Police Department and was the motorcycle officer in charge of the President's motorcycle escort that day. Officer Ellis testified before the Warren Commission and is listed in the index of the 26 volumes. The 26-volume index lists his testimony as being in Volume VII, starting on page 581, but his testimony is not there and I have been unable to find his testimony anywhere in the 26 volumes. I do not know why this officer's testimony, which would weigh heavily in favor of determining that it was the third shot that missed, was omitted from the Warren Report. When Officer Ellis was interviewed by Larry Snead for his book, NO MORE SILENCE, Officer Ellis stated that he was opposite the grassy knoll when he saw a bullet hit the curb and saw, "a bunch of junk flew up like a white or grey color dust coming out of the concrete." From Officer Ellis's position in the motorcade, for Officer Ellis to be opposite the grassy knoll when he saw the bullet hit the curb, President Kennedy had to have already been hit by the fatal headshot.

Royce Skelton, a railroad man, was standing on the triple underpass at the east railing and was looking down at the President's car as it was about to go under the triple underpass when he saw a bullet hit the curb. He testified, "I saw a bullet or I guess it was a bullet, I take for granted it was, hit in the left front of the President's car on the cement, and when it did, the smoke carried with it away from the building."

Charles Brehm was a decorated World War II veteran of the D-Day invasion and was personally honored by President Reagan on the 40th anniversary of D-day, and again personally honored by

President Clinton at the White House on the 50th anniversary of D-day. Charles Brehm was standing with his five-year-old son across Elm Street from the grassy knoll on November 22, 1963. Mr. Brehm was among those who were closest to the President's car when the headshot occurred. Mr. Brehm states he clearly saw the President's reaction to the first shot, then clearly saw the headshot in front of him and then heard a third shot after the first two shots. Mr. Brehm stated, "I do believe that shot (the third shot) went wild, it didn't hit anybody. I don't think it could have hit anybody."

Emmett J. Hudson was sitting on the steps on the north side of Elm Street about half-way up to the grassy knoll. These steps are the steps right in the middle of the grassy knoll. Mr. Hudson was another key witness to the fatal headshot, as it happened in front of him while he was looking directly at the President. Mr. Hudson was among those that were closest to the Presidential limousine at the moment of the fatal headshot. The F.B.I. and the Warren Commission were fully aware of Mr. Hudson and what he had to say about the missed shot because Mr. Hudson gave a statement to Sheriff's Deputies at the Sheriff's Office on November 22, 1963, immediately after the assassination of President Kennedy. The Warren Commission staff was about to close down their investigation of the assassination without ever calling Mr. Hudson to testify when it finally became public knowledge in June 1964 that one shot had missed the President's limousine. Mr. Hudson did testify on July 22, 1964, before Warren Commission Assistant Counsel Wesley J. Liebler. Hudson testified that he heard the first shot, though not realizing initially it was a shot. I then quote from Mr. Hudson's testimony: "When the second one rung out, the motorcade had done got further down Elm, and you see, I was trying to get a good look at President Kennedy. I happened to be looking right at him when that bullet hit him—the second shot." Mr. Hudson is then asked by Liebler, "Is it right that the second shot hit the President in the head?" and Mr. Hudson replied, "I know it was." Mr. Hudson was asked how many shots he heard and he replied that he heard three shots. Mr. Hudson is then asked by Liebeler, "And after you saw him hit in the head, did you hear another shot?" and Hudson replied, "Yes sir." Hudson is then asked by Liebeler, "Did you see that shot hit anything—the third shot?" Hudson replied, "No sir." Liebeler continued to question Hudson whether he was sure it was the second shot that hit the President in the head, and he then heard a third shot. Hudson did not waiver in his statement that he heard the third shot but did not see it hit anything after he saw the President hit in the head by a bullet. Up to this point in his testimony, the only thing Mr. Hudson had said about the first shot was, "The first shot rung out and, of course, I didn't realize it was a shot." Nevertheless, Liebeler did not give up, trying to put words in Hudson's mouth, and he continued with a series of questions that were obviously asked to confuse Mr. Hudson. Again, I quote from Hudson's Warren Commission testimony.

Mr. Liebeler: You say it was the second shot that hit him in the head?
Mr. Hudson: Yes.
Mr. Liebeler: What happened after the President got hit in the head, did you see what he did, what happened in the car?
Mr. Hudson: He slumped over and Mrs. Kennedy, she climbs over in the seat with him and pulls him over.
Mr. Liebeler: Pulled him down in the seat?
Mr. Hudson: Pulled him over in her lap like.

As you can see by his testimony up to this point, Mr. Hudson is positive about what he had witnessed and it fits with what was recorded on film in the Zapruder movie. Then the questioning shows what happened to many witnesses when they testified to something the Warren Commission staff lawyers did not want to hear. The staff lawyers misquote what the witness had just said to confuse the witness. Mr. Hudson had just testified he heard the first shot and saw the second shot hit the President in the head, and then heard a third shot. Commission Attorney Liebler ignored what Hudson had just testified to and continued his deposition of Hudson with a question that is not what Hudson had just stated. It worked to confuse Hudson for a few questions, but in the end, Hudson comes back to his original statement, that he heard another shot after seeing the second shot hit the President in the head. Here is a continuation of Liebler's confusing questions and Mr. Hudson's answers.

Mr. Liebeler: If you don't think the President got hit by the first shot and you say he got hit in the head by the second shot——
Mr. Hudson: Yes.
Mr. Liebeler: And if we assume that he was hit twice, you would have to say that he was hit by the third shot; isn't that right?
Mr. Hudson: Yes.
Mr. Liebeler: He was hit again after he got hit in the head?
Mr. Hudson: Yes sir.
Mr. Liebeler: Do you think that it could have been possible when Mrs. Kennedy pulled him over, do you think he could have got hit in the neck after he had been hit in the head?
Mr. Hudson: Yes sir, I do.
Liebeler: He was still sitting far enough up in the car he could have been hit?
Mr. Hudson: Yes sir.

Liebeler then asks Hudson a series of questions about pictures taken, and the location of the President's car during the shooting, asking Hudson to try and identify himself in those pictures. Then, once again, Liebeler goes back to the headshot.

Liebeler: And you had already heard one shot when you saw the President get hit in the head?
Mr. Hudson: Yes.
Mr. Liebeler: And you heard another shot after that time?
Mr. Hudson: Yes.

One must remember that the Dealey Plaza witnesses, including myself, heard a delay between the first and second shots and then heard the crack of two high-powered rifle shots in quick succession. The third shot was a hurried shot and it missed its mark entirely.

There are many other witnesses whose statements more than indicate that it was the third shot that went wild and hit the curb. When you study all of these witness testimonies, put all of their testimony together, and add my personal knowledge, the overwhelming fact is that the third shot missed the President's limousine and hit the curb near where I was standing by the triple underpass and sent a shower of debris into my face. The third shot was the missed shot.

GOVERNOR CONNALLY'S WOUNDS

The wounds that Governor John Connally received during the shooting are one of the main centers for controversy in the Warren Report. The Governor was hit in the back by a bullet near the right armpit. The bullet struck a rib, shattering the rib, and exited just below his right nipple. This bullet or another then shattered his right wrist and penetrated his thigh, leaving a fragment near the bone. The Governor survived these wounds and the Warren Commission determined that Governor Connally was hit by the same bullet that hit President Kennedy in the back. The Warren Commission staff used a faulty artist drawing that placed the President's back wound six inches too high for the Governor to have been hit by the same bullet. The Governor was also too far to the right of the President's so-called throat exit wound to have been hit near the right armpit. A pristine bullet found at Parkland Hospital after rolling off a stretcher was determined by the Warren Commission staff to be the bullet that caused both men's wounds, though the bullet found at Parkland had no fragments missing. Every test attempted to duplicate the Governor's wounds resulted in a mutilated bullet. The Zapruder amateur movie shows that the Governor did not react to being hit until a second or two after the President was hit in the back. Governor Connally testified before the Warren Commission that he was hit by a different bullet than the one that hit the President. He remembers hearing the first shot, turning to his right to try to see the President behind him and not being able to do so, then turning back to his left when he was hit. The Governor's wife, Nellie, testified to the same thing. The Zapruder movie confirms the Governor's and his wife's testimony. Governor Connally never changed his testimony as long as he lived. The Warren Commission's theory of a single bullet hitting both men will not hold water. The only other explanation is that there was a second gunman shooting from the rear, and that would mean there was a conspiracy to kill the President. I do not have a ready answer, nor can I give an explanation of how Governor Connally was wounded. The wounding of Governor Connally is part of why we will never know the truth about the assassination of President John F. Kennedy.

MAKE THE EVIDENCE FIT

There is example after example of how evidence was altered or changed to make it fit a predetermined outcome. There could be hundreds of pages written about all the examples of this in the investigation of the assassination of President Kennedy. The autopsy was one example of making the evidence fit. I touched on the autopsy in an earlier chapter, but let us take a look at just one portion of the autopsy—how it was determined that the throat wound was found to be an exit wound. The autopsy doctors completely missed the throat wound during the autopsy. They were well into the autopsy when they turned the President's body over to examine the President's back, which is when they discovered a bullet hole in the back about six inches below the collar line. Dr. Humes probed this wound with his finger and determined that the wound had a downward trajectory of 45 to 60 degrees. He also found that he could only probe the wound an inch or so and his finger could touch the end of the opening. Drs. Boswell and Finck were assisting Dr. Humes and they also probed the back wound and found that they could only probe the wound an inch or so to feel the end of the opening. They then probed the opening with a metal probe, a thin piece of stiff metal with a small ball on the end some eight inches long. The metal probe also could only go into the wound an inch or so. There were Naval Brass, medical technicians, F.B.I. agents, and Secret Service Agents watching the doctors probe this wound. Secret Service Agent Roy Kellerman testified to the Warren Commission that he finally spoke up and asked Dr. Finck, "Colonel, where did it go?" and the doctor replied, "There are no lanes for outlet of this entry." Dr. Humes later told the Warren Commission "attempts to probe the wound were unsuccessful without fear of making a false passage." According to other witnesses at the autopsy, the doctors were confused because there was no exit for this wound and no bullet to be found. At about 11 P.M., the autopsy was over and the doctors concluded that one missile entered the back of the President and was apparently dislodged during cardiac massage at Parkland Hospital.

The next morning, Saturday, November 23, 1963, with his autopsy report already made out, Commander Humes called Parkland Hospital in Dallas and spoke to Dr. Malcolm Perry who had attended to the President the day before. In the course of that conversation, Dr. Humes learned from Dr. Perry that there had been a bullet wound in the President's throat and that the Parkland doctors had performed a tracheotomy at that spot. Commander Humes left Bethesda Naval Hospital carrying the autopsy notes from the night before and went home. At home, he rewrote the official autopsy report, which included the finding of a wound in the President's throat. Dr. Humes then burned the original autopsy report. As Dr. Humes rewrote the autopsy report after learning of the throat wound, the President's body was lying in state at the White House.

More than a decade later, Dr. Humes was called to testify before the House Select Committee. He testified that when Dr. Perry told him about the throat wound "lights went on, and we said, ah, we have some place for our missile to have gone." The entrance wound in the President's throat that the Parkland doctors had observed was now officially an exit wound. A back entrance wound six inches below the collar was now in the shoulder near the collar line. A back wound that had had a downward slant of 45 to 60 degrees was now more horizontal so that the bullet could come out the throat. Two days later, Dr. Humes orally instructed an artist regarding how to draw the back wound for the Warren Commission in the neck so it would be higher than the throat "exit" wound. Dr. Humes evidently forgot to put the back wound up in the shoulder on the autopsy report. He also evidently did not realize that the President's coat and shirt with bullet holes six inches below the collar would also be evidence. As you can see, it was not at all hard to make the evidence fit. Just an example of why we will never know the truth about the assassination.

THE ZAPRUDER FILM

Abraham Zapruder was a Dallas businessman whose office was near Dealey Plaza at 501 Elm Street in Dallas. He had decided to go to Dealey Plaza with his 8mm camera to film President Kennedy's motorcade on November 22, 1963, but little did he know that he was about to take the amateur movie of the century. When the motorcade rounded the corner of Houston and Elm Streets in front of the Texas Schoolbook Depository, Mr. Zapruder was standing on a ledge that was part of the Pergola at the rear of the grassy knoll. He had his secretary to help steady him so he would not fall. Mr. Zapruder started his camera rolling as the President's limousine turned the corner onto Elm and continued filming until the President's car went under the triple underpass.

Immediately after the shooting, Abraham Zapruder walked back to his office and called the F.B.I. He then went to nearby WFAA-TV and did a live interview with Jay Watson. From there, he was accompanied by Forrest V. Sorrels, head of the Secret Service in Dallas, to the Eastman Kodak Company at 3131 Manor Way in Dallas to have the film developed. The film was developed and the identification number 0183 was made part of the film. Eastman Kodak did not have a way to duplicate the developed movie at that office, but did recommend Jamieson Film Company at 3825 Bryan Street in Dallas to have copies made. Zapruder and Sorrels then went to Jamieson where three duplicate copies were made. They then returned to Mr. Zapruder's office and viewed the film as many as 15 times; it was now about 4 P.M. The original and at least one copy were then flown to Washington D.C. that same evening, November 22, 1963, and delivered to the National Photographic Interpretation Center in Suitland, Maryland, whose employees are paid by the C.I.A. Ben Hunter and Homer A, McMahon, employees of N.P.I.C., were called at home to come and do work on the film. The Secret Service courier, a Capt. Sands, told them the original film and the copies were developed by Kodak at Eastman Kodak in Rochester, New York. (Yes, that is what these two men were positive they were told by Sands when interviewed in 1997 by the Assassination Records Review Board, that Rochester Kodak had developed the film, not Dallas Kodak.) The original and the copies were in the hands of N.P.I.C. until about 3 A.M. EST and arrived back in Dallas at about 6:30 A.M. CST Saturday morning, November 23, 1963. The original film was delivered back to Mr. Zapruder at his office at approximately 7 A.M., and sometime after 8 A.M. CST, the film rights were sold to Life Magazine. The movie was then shown to a group of reporters in Mr. Zapruder's office, including Dan Rather of CBS. Life Magazine published 31 frames of this amateur movie in their November 29th issue.

At one time, the Abraham Zapruder 8mm amateur movie taken in Dealey Plaza on November 22, 1963 was thought to be the best evidence of the assassination of President John F. Kennedy and the wounding of Governor John Connally. The Zapruder film was what the Warren Commission used to determine the timing of the shots, direction of the shots, and other vital information to determine that Lee Harvey Oswald was the lone assassin. Credible researchers over the years have pointed out flaws in this amateur movie suspecting alterations and finding inconsistencies with eyewitness reports and other pictures taken at the same moment. The Assassination Records Review Board (ARRB), a government-funded program to preserve the assassination records, did extensive work in the 90's on this amateur movie and determined that there are indeed problems with the film. There are at least 24 versions in different formats. The so-called original version that was sold to Life Magazine, the Secret Service version, the F.B.I. version, the C.I.A. version, and other versions are different. There is a preponderance of evidence that the movie has been tampered with. There are frames missing, splices in the film, and the unique original perforated I.D. marking 0183 is not on the so-called original today. The head wound as shown in the Zapruder movie is not consistent with Dealey Plaza witnesses, motorcade witnesses, or Parkland hospital witnesses. There is a dark spot at the back of the head in the movie where witnesses saw brain debris exit from the rear of the President's head. The movie shows the debris going up and slightly forward with the right side of the President's head exploding. Most importantly, this debris is only shown in two frames, while it would take a minimum of three or more frames for this debris to go up and start dissipating as it is coming back down. The background images are not consistent with a moving vehicle, as both are in focus. If the camera is moving while filming a moving vehicle, the background images will be blurry and out of focus while the vehicle is clear. On the other hand, if the camera is stationary, the background will be clear while the moving vehicle will be blurry and out of focus. There are those who say that because both the vehicle and the background are clear it is evidence that the limousine had stopped, but the limousine does not stop in the Zapruder movie. There are people in one place in one frame and a few feet away in the next frame. The secret service agent driving the car turns his head in one frame and in the next frame it is 110 degrees different, something that is not humanly possible in one-eighteenth of a second. The blinking lights of the Presidential limousine are also out of sync in the movie because of missing frames. There is a long list of such abnormalities. One needs to view the movie frame by frame to find these abnormalities, but they are there. Today, 40 years later, even the authenticity of the altered original Zapruder amateur movie taken on November 22, 1963 cannot be verified. There is overwhelming and undisputable evidence that the Zapruder film has been tampered with. I was able to obtain a bootleg 8mm copy of the so-called original 8mm Zapruder movie in the late 60's, long before the movie became public, and I still have that copy today. I have the late 60's bootleg copy and later copies and there is a difference. If you take the Zapruder film as being authentic, and frames of it have to be, there are still problems found. The film shows in graphic detail the fatal shot that rips President Kennedy's head apart. The frames showing the fatal shot, supposedly a single shot coming from the rear, from the Schoolbook Depository building according to the Warren Commission, show the President's head and body being thrown violently backward and slammed into the back of the seat of the limousine. This is contrary to all laws of physics. The impact of a bullet shot from a high powered rifle will force the object that is hit to move violently away from the source of the shot, not draw the object toward that source. However a shot fired from behind the picket fence at the back of the grassy knoll, would have the exact result that is shown in the Zapruder film head shot, the head and body are blown away from the source of the shot, to the rear and to the left as the sequence of frames in the movie show. It is strong evidence that there was in fact a frontal shot, and at least two shooters. At first the authorities attributed this violent snap backward to the limousine's rapid acceleration, but this theory was quickly debunked when other photographs showed that the limousine had in reality almost come to a stop after the headshot. Then two new theories were soon advanced to explain why in this instance, the head and body violently reacted toward the direction of the shot. One was a "neuro reaction" and the other a "jet" effect. A careful study of the Zapruder movie does not give credibility to either of these theories.

Why was the Zapruder film placed in the hands of C.I.A. photographic employees that night and then sent back to Dallas the next morning? Abraham Zapruder's business partner was one of the persons who viewed the film after it was developed on November 22, 1963, and then viewed the film again the next morning when Life Magazine was bargaining for the rights to the movie. He remarked that the movie seemed different than when he had viewed it yesterday.

THE PSEUDO SECRET SERVICE AGENTS

Gordon Arnold was on leave from the Army, and he planned to take motion pictures of the motorcade from the railroad tracks on top of the triple underpass. Arnold was wearing his U.S. Army uniform as he proceeded behind the picket fence toward railroad tracks on top of the triple overpass. He was soon approached by a man in civilian clothes wearing a sidearm, and the man told Arnold he was not allowed up there. Arnold challenged the man's authority, and the man then pulled out a badge, saying he was with the Secret Service and did not want anyone up there. Arnold then took up another position in Dealey Plaza. Joe Marshall Smith was a seven-year Dallas Police veteran. On November 22, 1963, he was assigned to the Corner of Elm and Houston Streets. One of his assignments was to stop traffic on Elm Street when the President's motorcade arrived at that intersection. When the first shot rang out, Officer Smith was in the middle of Elm Street on the East edge of Houston Street holding up traffic. Officer Smith testified before the Warren Commission on July 23, 1964, stating: "This woman came up to me and she was in hysterics. She told me, 'They are shooting the President from the bushes.'" Officer Smith ran to the area immediately behind the concrete structure at the top of the grassy knoll and started checking the bushes and the cars in the parking lot. He encountered a man behind the picket fence, who upon seeing Smith produced Secret Service credentials without being asked. Officer Smith allowed this man to go on his way. The Secret Service denied they had an agent in that area at that time.

Sergeant D. V. Harkness was a 17-year Dallas Police veteran. On November 22, 1963, he was the officer in charge of the traffic officers along the parade route. He was at the corner of Main and

Houston Streets when the shots rang out. Sergeant Harkness testified before the Warren Commission on April 9, 1964. His testimony shows that when he observed the President's car almost come to a stop he got on his motorcycle and went west on Main Street to between the triple underpass and Industrial to see if anyone was fleeing that area. When he saw no one, he then went to the area behind the picket fence where he ran into Amos Euins who told him the shots came from the Schoolbook Depository. He took Amos Euins to Inspector Sawyer's car in front of the Depository and then went to the back of the Depository to seal the back entrance area. At the rear of the building, Sergeant Harkness encountered "some Secret Service Agents there. I didn't get them identified. They told me they were Secret Service." In separate testimony from the Secret Service, it was firmly established that of the 28 Secret Service Agents in Dallas that day, not one agent was in the grassy knoll area or the parking lot behind the grassy knoll and no agent was on foot in the area before or after the shooting. Later that afternoon one lone agent did go into the Schoolbook Depository. The Dallas Police radio communication tapes show that Sergeant Harkness radioed in about Euins being a witness six minutes after the shooting. For Sergeant Harkness to run into the so-called "Secret Service Agents" and seal off the building, it had to be at least two or three minutes later, eight or nine minutes after the shooting.

ODD FELLOWS

There have been many stories written about the odd assortment of shady characters who were in or near Dealey Plaza on November 22, 1963, at the very time President John F. Kennedy was assassinated. Some were taken into custody and questioned, and if they gave a somewhat reasonable answer as to why they were there, they were released without any record being kept of who they were. Some were later identified in some of the hundreds of pictures taken that day and their backgrounds raised questions. Some were never identified. What most of them had in common was that there was not a serious investigation by any investigative agency as to why they were there at that particular moment in time.

Jim Braden was one of those in Dealey Plaza that day. Mr. Braden was taken into custody moments after the shooting as he came out of the Dal-Tex building just east of the Schoolbook Depository. The Dal-Tex building has a clear view down Elm Street to the triple underpass and many critics have claimed that shots could have also been fired from this building. An elevator operator had noticed that Mr. Braden was a stranger in the building and summoned Deputy Sheriff C. L. Lewis. Mr. Braden was taken to the Sheriff's office when he produced only a credit card for identification. There he was interrogated and gave a statement that he was in Dallas on oil business. Mr. Braden said he was walking down Elm Street trying to catch a taxi but there were none. He then asked someone where he might find a phone and was told there was one on the third floor of the Dal-Tex building. He stated the phone on the third floor did not work and he was leaving the building when he was stopped. Mr. Braden's explanation of why he was in the Dal-Tex building was accepted by the Sheriff's office, and once his statement was typed and he signed it, he was released. Mr. Braden used a Beverly Hills, California address. Jim Braden was in reality Eugene Hale Brading, a career criminal who had started using the Jim Braden alias a few months earlier. Mr. Brading had an F.B.I. rap sheet that listed three dozen arrests, and he had felony convictions in several states for burglary, embezzlement, mail fraud, and conspiracy.

According to witnesses, another young man was led from the Dal-Tex building by police wearing a leather coat and leather gloves, despite it being a mild Texas day. There is no record of who this man was or what happened to him. Photographs show another man being searched by police as he left the Dal-Tex building. This man claimed he wandered into the Dal-Tex building looking for a phone, and when he found that all the lines were busy, he started to leave but was stopped by police. He was taken to the Sheriff's office and released. There is no record as to who he was.

The most famous of those taken into custody that day are the three tramps. They were discovered in a boxcar in the railroad yard behind the grassy knoll. As they were being marched off to the Sheriff's office, several photographs were taken of them. At first glance they have a bedraggled look, but critics have pointed out that two of the tramps only have the appearance of being tramps. Their shoes are in good repair and thick-soled, their hair has been recently barbered, they are freshly shaven, and a close inspection of their clothing shows that it is only wrinkled, not ragged. Many assassination researchers, including noted Washington columnist Jack Anderson, believed that the tall tramp is actor Woody Harrelson's father, Charles Voyd Harrelson, an organized crime hit man convicted in 1979 for the murder of United States District Court Judge, John H. Wood Jr. Charles Harrelson is serving a life term in Federal prison for Judge Wood's murder. They were fingerprinted, mug shots were taken, and then the men were released. The fingerprints and mug shots have disappeared with no record of their names, what they were doing there, or where they came from. Many critics believe that with their position behind the picket fence, even if they had nothing to do with the killing, the three tramps might have witnessed something that could contribute to the investigation.

In an F.B.I. report dated the next day, November 23, 1963, Marvin C. Robinson reported that he was driving west on Elm Street. As soon as Elm Street opened up after the motorcade passed, he started through Dealey Plaza in heavy traffic and he saw a light-colored Nash station wagon stop in front of the Schoolbook depository. Mr. Robinson reported that a white man walked down the grassy incline and got into the station wagon.

Deputy Sheriff Roger Craig also made a statement about the Nash station wagon: "I heard a shrill whistle and I turned around and saw a white male running down the hill from the direction of the Schoolbook Depository Building, and I saw what I think was a light-colored Rambler station wagon (Nash made Rambler) with a luggage rack on top pull over to the curb and this subject who had come running down the hill got into the car. The man driving this station wagon was a dark-complected white male. I tried to get across Elm Street to stop the car and talk with the subjects, but the traffic was so heavy I could not make it."

Richard Randolph Carr, a steel worker, also saw a man get into a Nash Rambler. Mr. Carr stated the man driving the Nash Rambler was "real dark- complected" and appeared to be Spanish or Cuban. It must be noted that through the years Mr. Carr's recall has been somewhat inconsistent since his original statement. He has been intimidated, shot at, and dynamite has been found wired to his car's ignition. Yet, his basic statement that he saw a man get into a Rambler station wagon was consistent.

There are photographs that were taken right after the assassination that show a light-colored Nash Rambler station wagon with a luggage rack on the top moving along in traffic in Dealey Plaza.

Then there is the famous "umbrella man." The weather in Dallas that day was sunny and warm, but one man had an open umbrella. Pictures taken that day show he was standing near the curb on the north side of Elm Street, and as the President's limousine approached where he was standing, he raised the umbrella high over his head and the first shot was fired, the shot that hit the President in the back. He then walked off. There was much speculation that this man, in raising his umbrella at that very moment, was a signal to start the shooting and kill the President. All efforts to identify this man failed for 15 years. Then a recognizable picture of his face appeared in newspapers across the country. Someone recognized him as Louis Witt. Witt was found and was unaware that he had been the subject of a 15-year search. When asked about his raising the umbrella, he replied that he did not like Kennedy and that he raised his umbrella in protest of Kennedy.

ONE PLOT FOILED...OR WAS IT?

The F.B.I. had a long file on Joseph Milteer, an extreme right-wing political organizer and a racist. Milteer had inherited a large sum of money, had no family, did not work, and traveled extensively to attend various radical right-wing meetings. Milteer devoted his life to right-wing causes; he belonged to at least four right-wing organizations—The National States Right Party, The Dixie Klan, The Constitution Party, and The White Citizens Counsel. When he was home, he wrote articles that blasted Kennedy, Jews, Communists, the UN, local politicians, and the Federal Government.

President Kennedy had planned a trip to Miami, Florida for November 18, 1963, and a motorcade was planned for this visit. On Saturday November 9, 1963, two friends met for breakfast—one was Joseph Milteer and one was a union organizer, Willie Somersett. The Miami Police and the F.B.I. had recruited Somersett to be an undercover informant on Milteer because Milteer detested President Kennedy. Somersett had set up a tape recorder to tape their conversation and soon they were talking about President Kennedy and his scheduled visit to Miami. The taped conversation went as follows:

Somersett: I think Kennedy is coming here on the 18th to make some kind of speech, I imagine it will be on TV.
Milteer: You can bet your bottom dollar he is going to have a lot to say about the Cubans, there are so many of them here.
Somersett: Yeah, well he will have a thousand bodyguards. Don't worry about that.
Milteer: The more bodyguards he has, the easier it is to get him.
Somersett: What?
Milteer: The more bodyguards he has the more easier it is to get him.
Somersett: Well, how in the hell do you figure would be the best way to get him?
Milteer: From an office building with a high-powered rifle. How many people does he have going around who look just like him. Do you know about that?
Somersett: No, I never heard he had anybody.

Milteer: He has about fifteen. Whenever ho goes anyplace, he knows he is a marked man.
Somersett: You think he knows he is a marked man?
Milteer: Sure he does.
Somersett: They are really going to try to kill him?
Milteer: Oh, yeah, it is in the works.
Somersett: Hitting this Kennedy is going to be a hard proposition, I tell you. I believe you may have figured out a way to get to him, the office building and all of that. I don't know how the Secret Service agents cover all of them office buildings everywhere he is going. Do you know whether they do that or not?
Milteer: Well, if they have any suspicion they do that, of course. But without any suspicion, chances are that they wouldn't. You take there in Washington. This is the wrong time of the year, but in pleasant weather, he comes out on the veranda and somebody could be in a hotel room across the way and pick him off just like that.
Somersett: Is that right?
Milteer: Sure, disassemble a gun. You don't have to take a gun up there, you can take it up in pieces. All those guns come knock down. You can take them apart. Well, we are going to have to get nasty.
Somersett: Yeah, get nasty.
Milteer: We have got to be ready, we have got to be sitting on go, too.
Somersett: Yeah, that is right.
Milteer: There ain't any countdown to it, we have just got to be sitting on go, Countdown, they can move in on you, and on go they can't. Countdown is alright for a slow prepared operation. But in an emergency operation, you have got to be sitting on go.
Somersett: Boy, if that Kennedy gets shot, we have got to know where we are at. Because you know that will be a real shake.
Milteer: They wouldn't leave any stone unturned there. No way. They will pick up somebody within hours afterwards, if anything like that would happen, just to throw the public off, if anything like that would happen, just to throw the public off.
Somersett: Oh, somebody is going to have to go to jail, if he gets killed.
Milteer: Just like Bruno Hauptman in the Lindbergh case, you know.

The next day Willie Somersett turned the tape over to Miami Police Chief Walter Headley and Detective Sergeant Charles Sapp. After the Miami Police listened to the tape, they notified the F.B.I. The F.B.I. updated its files on Milteer, and on November 17, 1963, the F.B.I. sent a telex to all SACs (Special Agents in Charge) nationwide that "the bureau has determined that a militant revolutionary group may attempt to assassinate President Kennedy on his proposed trip to Dallas, Texas." The Secret Service was also notified and President Kennedy's motorcade in Miami was cancelled. After President John F. Kennedy was assassinated, Milteer and Somersett met again at the Union Train Station in Jacksonville Florida at about 4:25 P.M. on November 23, 1963. This meeting was not taped, but Somersett reported that Milteer was enthusiastic that Kennedy was dead and said, "I told you so, it happened just like I told you, a high-powered rifle from a window, that is the way it was supposed to be done."

Milteer's reference to Bruno Hauptman in the Lindbergh case was that many thought that Hauptman was wrongly convicted of kidnapping the Lindbergh baby, and that so much public pressure had been put on the police that they had to find someone, anyone, to convict of the crime.

The controversy over whether Joseph Milteer had prior knowledge of the assassination of President Kennedy or was just a blowhard has gone on for years. It is known that Milteer contacted

Robert Shelton of the United Klans of America, Knights of the Ku Klux Klan, the evening before the black Baptist Church on 16th Street in Birmingham, Alabama was bombed and black children killed. Even Milteer's death is controversial. The death certificate lists cause of death as severe burns to his lower limbs; however, the mortician who attended to Milteer said the burns were minor and almost healed when he died. There was no autopsy.

There is no mention of Joseph Milteer in the Warren Report that I can find. However, documents discovered in the National Archives years later show evidence that the Warren Commission was aware of Milteer.

WAS THERE A COVER-UP?

It would be wrong for me to make a blanket statement that the Warren Report was a cover-up. The F.B.I. made 25,000 reports regarding the assassination from November 22, 1963 until September 1964, and approximately 9,000 of those F.B.I. reports were given to the Warren Commission staff. One must remember that it was the 14 staff lawyers who did the majority of the work, not the seven members of the Warren Commission. The seven members of the Warren Commission made decisions on what to use in the report from the summaries given to them by the staff. There is plenty of evidence that there was bickering, disagreement, and a show of temperament amongst the staff. With all of the depositions taken from witnesses, the staff had little time to fully study the 9,000 F.B.I. reports. They were also under pressure from the public, the press, and the White House to get the report out. I only had contact with two of the Warren Commission staff lawyers. Wesley Liebler took my deposition; he was polite and made a good impression on me. I met another staff lawyer when we rode to the airport together after we both appeared on a talk show in New York City. I tried to make small talk with him and asked him how he happened to get on the staff. He then proceeded to tell me how important he was. When I asked him how staff lawyer Arlen Spector arrived at the single bullet theory, that one bullet hit both President Kennedy and Governor Connally, he snapped at me in a child-like manner and said "that was my idea, and not Spector's." When I asked him why the Commission had for six months ignored the missed shot that hit near me, he glared at me, turned to look out the window, and never said another word to me on the way to the airport. He just sat there with a pouting expression on his face. I can only assume that the staff lawyers were like everyone else, that some took their job seriously and others let their ego interfere with their work.

I can find little fault with the seven Commission members. They were handicapped and working under the predetermined conclusions that F.B.I Director J. Edgar Hoover had laid out for them. They also had to work with staff lawyers who, as a whole, had little investigative experience. To their credit, they questioned and disagreed with many of the staff's conclusions. They were aware of the problem with F.B.I. Director J. Edgar Hoover, and tried to work around it. The one problem I do have is with Representative Gerald Ford, who was to later become President Ford. The Commission's meetings were supposed to be secret. Documents uncovered years later reveal that Representative Ford reported to the F.B.I. after each of their Commission meetings regarding what was discussed. In those meetings, the Commission would have questions and decide to ask Hoover about their questions. The next morning before they had a chance to make a request for their questions there would be an answer from Hoover answering their questions. Gerald Ford kept J. Edgar Hoover informed about every thing that was going on with the Warren Commission. With the circumstances the Warren Commission and its staff worked under, it is a miracle that we got the report that we did.

Was there a cover-up? I can only answer that question about my own personal experience and from what I have learned through the years. The answer is yes, a definite yes, a 100% yes; there was a cover-up by the F.B.I. in regard to one shot completely missing and hitting the curb near me. When I say F.B.I., I am not talking about the average Special Agent working out in the field. I am talking about the upper echelon that controlled the reports that these honest, hard-working F.B.I. agents made. Twelve known witnesses gave statements or testified that they saw the bullet hit the curb and debris fly up. When some of the witnesses tried to bring up the missed shot hitting the curb during their deposition, it is obvious that the staff lawyer taking their deposition was surprised by what they were trying to say and was unfamiliar with what they were trying to say. Within minutes after the assassination, Deputy Sheriff Buddy Walthers located where the bullet had hit the curb and left a scar (see page 165). At 12:37 P.M., seven minutes after the assassination, it was called in by police that one man had been hit by debris from a missed shot. During the next few minutes, Deputy Walthers took several of his fellow deputies to the spot and showed them the scar on the curb. It became instant common knowledge in the Sheriff's department that one bullet missed. Homicide Detective Gus Rose took my statement that afternoon, and that statement was never to be seen again. Tom Dillard, chief photographer for the DALLAS MORNING NEWS, took photographs of the curb. Jim Underwood, a television photographer, also took pictures of the scar on the curb. Two articles appeared in the Dallas papers about the missed shot (documents show that the F.B.I. clipped and saved every article about the assassination). I was interviewed by two F.B.I. agents three weeks after the assassination. Then silence, nothing. Years later we learned from the forced release of F.B.I. documents under the Freedom of Information Act that in early F.B.I. reports on interviews with Tom Dillard, Jim Underwood, Deputy Buddy Walthers, and other Sheriff's deputies there is no mention of a missed shot. Then on June 5, 1964, nearly six months after the assassination, I tell Jim Lehrer, at that time a reporter for the DALLAS TIMES HERALD about the missed shot. When Jim Lehrer put this story about a missed shot during the shooting on the wire services, at my request not using my name, Mr. Lehrer received several calls wanting to know who I was. One of the calls was from someone within the Warren Commission. The fact that one shot had missed the President's limousine was now public knowledge. The F.B.I. acted immediately and had two agents in Jim Lehrer's office by 4:00 P.M. that after noon. That F.B.I. report demonized me as someone seeking publicity and money. J. Edgar Hoover then wrote a memo to J. Lee Rankin, Chief Counsel for the Warren Commission, that the F.B.I. knew about me all along and about my "claim" of a missed shot and that they had interviewed me in December of 1963. When J. Lee Rankin asked Hoover to find the spot where the bullet hit the curb, Hoover reported that there was no mark to be found on the curb. J. Lee Rankin had Assistant U. S. Attorney Martha Jo Stroud in Dallas attain pictures of the curb scar from Tom Dillard and Jim Underwood. With pictures of the curb scar, Rankin told Hoover to locate the mark. The mark was soon found by the F.B.I., and I was at last called to testify before the Warren Commission. More than eight months after the assassination of the President, the curb section was cut out of the street on August 5, 1964 and sent to the F.B.I. laboratory for a spectrographic analysis (see pages 166 and 167). Once the analysis was completed, Hoover sent a memo to Rankin saying that traces of lead and antimony were found, but no trace of copper. Without copper it could not have been a whole bullet that hit the curb. The Warren Commission disregarded Hoover's comment about no trace of copper, however, and concluded that it was a missed shot, a whole bullet that hit the curb. Years later, after the F.B.I. was forced to turn over their documents under the Freedom of Information Act, a document was discovered that stated there were two pieces of President Kennedy's clothing that had also undergone spectrographic analysis and there was no trace of copper around the bullet holes in these articles of clothing either. After years of having Harold Weisberg tell me the mark on the curb had been patched, in 1997 I decided to go to the National Archives and see for myself. The curb section had been stored in the archives for safekeeping and Harold had examined the curb in the 70's. Harold had also sued the F.B.I. under the Freedom of Information Act for release of the wafer thin spectrographic analysis film to get a separate opinion on the results. The suit dragged on for years with the F.B.I lawyers vigorously fighting release of the wafer thin plate. The F.B.I. lawyers finally announced in the courtroom that the wafer thin plate had been thrown away to make room for storage. When I went to the Archives to examine the mark on the curb, I was armed with a high-powered magnifying glass, but I did not need it. You could see the mark had been patched with the naked eye. The Archives' assistant manager exclaimed to me, "I can see it has been patched." While at the Archives, I obtained a photograph of the curb that was taken just before the curb section was cut out of the street on August 5, 1964. The photograph (see page 166) revealed that the curb had been patched before it was cut out of the street and the patchwork was visible to the naked eye. After leaving the Archives, I drove to Harold's house in Frederick, Maryland. Harold gave me an engineering report made by a respected engineering firm that was ordered by one of the foremost and best known magazines in America. The engineering report was dated in 1983, and the report determined that the curb had been patched at some time. Every piece of evidence that I have been able to obtain in the last 40 years points directly at J. Edgar Hoover, Director of the F.B.I., as being responsible for trying to cover up that one shot fired during the assassination of President Kennedy went astray and hit the curb in front of me, spraying debris into my face.

Scar on curb indicated with tip of pen. Photo Tom Dillard.

A picture of the patched curb before it was cut out by the F.B.I.

Photo of the curb section stored in the National Archives.

This is an F.B.I. photo taken on 8/5/64 from the point where the missed shot hit the curb, just before the curb section was cut from the street. I was standing just to the left of this point on 11/22/63. The building in the center with the Hertz sign on top is the Schoolbook Depository. Three spent cartridges were found at the far right and second window down from the top. The building to the right of the Schoolbook Depository is the Dal-Tex building where some thought shots were fired from the fire escape stairs. The building on the far right is the Dallas County Jail and Sheriff's office. The picket fence can be seen to the left at the top of the grassy knoll. Abraham Zapruder filmed the assassination from a point behind the traffic sign on the left.

SMOKE AND OSWALD IN NEW ORLEANS

The Government's investigation into the assassination of President Kennedy started out with a string of bad luck fires right after the assassination. The last interview a Federal Agent had with Lee Harvey Oswald went up in smoke. The only notes taken during Oswald's interrogation at the Dallas Police Station apparently went up in smoke. A secret Oswald C.I.A. memo made before the assassination went up in smoke while being thermofaxed (copied). The original autopsy notes made by the autopsy pathologist went up in smoke in the doctor's own fireplace. When Lee Harvey Oswald was himself the third murder victim in Dallas in two days, after the murders of President Kennedy and Dallas Police Officer J. D. Tippit, F.B.I. Director J. Edgar Hoover took things into his own hands and decided to create his own smoke. Hoover sent out an internal F.B.I memo, stamped SECRET, to his department chiefs two days after the assassination of President Kennedy; the memo stated, "we will use the prestige of the F.B.I. to convince the American public that Oswald is the real assassin." Hoover did just that in his report to President Johnson of December 9, 1963, declaring Oswald to be the lone assassin and that there were three shots, three hits, no conspiracy, case closed. There was too much smoke in New Orleans, however, to put the fire out. New Orleans District Attorney Jim Garrison stumbled on evidence of a conspiracy a couple of years after the assassination. Garrison had just enough evidence to make him dangerous, but not enough to go to trial with, and it ended up making a fool out of Garrison. The movie JFK is based on Jim Garrison's investigation. Though the movie has a lot of proven facts in it, as in most movies of this type, there are just enough untruths that make the movie mere entertainment. I found it interesting when Kevin Costner, who played Jim Garrison in the movie, was summing up his case before the jury, he said the government had a neat tidy case all sewed up except for two things, "the Abraham Zapruder movie and James T. Tague." I was at first embarrassed by my name being used in the movie that way, but not anymore.

Lee Harvey Oswald was born in New Orleans in 1939. Oswald attended Beauregard Junior High School in 1955 when he was a teenager and joined the Civil Air Patrol. David Ferrie was a captain in that Civil Air Patrol. Oswald also spent most of the summer of 1963 in New Orleans. On August 9, 1963, Oswald was arrested for disturbing the peace; he had been handing out Fair Play for Cuba Committee literature when he got into a fight with Carlos Bringuier and two other Cubans in the 700 block of Canal Street in New Orleans. The leaflets were pro-Castro with a return address of 544 Camp Street, New Orleans, Louisiana. This was the address of an anti-Castro group, not a pro-Castro one. All evidence indicates Oswald himself printed the literature and was the only "member" of the Fair Play for Cuba Committee in New Orleans. Confusing? No, not when you find out the anti-Castro group listed on the return address was backed by the C.I.A. There is evidence that a pro-Castro cover was being created for Oswald.

When Oswald was in New Orleans in the summer of 1963, his case was handled by F.B.I. Special Agent Milton R. Kaack. In a report of October 31, 1963, Kaack wrote, "NO T-1 is an employ of the Federal government, NO T-1 is an employ of another government agency." An earlier Kaack report had stated, "Confidential informant NO T-1 advised on July 23, 1963, that post office box 30061 was rented by L. H. Oswald on June 5, 1963. He furnished as his address 657 French Street, New Orleans, Louisiana. T-1 advised on October 25, 1963, that the subject sent a forwarding address for P.O. Box 30061 on September 26, 1963, of 2515 West Fifth Street, Irving, Texas." Initially the Warren Commission thought T-1 was a Postal Inspector and asked Dallas Postal Inspector Harry D. Holmes to check it out. Holmes could not connect T-1 to anyone in the Postal Service, but did discover that still another change-of-address card was sent to the New Orleans Post Office on October 11 and it was postmarked in New Orleans. Oswald was in Dallas on October 11, 1963. When the Warren Commission staff could not come up with an answer to this puzzle, Assistant Counsel Wesley J. Liebler frankly admitted the problem and said, "Well, in any event we will add it to the pile." The October 31 Kaack report also mentions NO T-2, NO T-5, and NO T-6 as reporting on Oswald's activities in New Orleans. F.B.I. Agent Milton R. Kaack was not asked to testify to the Warren Commission. Someone in the Federal Government had a deep interest in Lee Harvey Oswald that went far beyond the F.B.I.

A little bit of background: Lee Harvey Oswald was given an Honorable Discharge from the United States Marines on September 11, 1959. The reason given for the discharge was a hardship to take care of his mother. The Warren Commission did not paint a good picture of Oswald's Marine Corps career. He was court-martialed twice, once for pouring a drink on a superior's head and once for accidentally injuring himself with a 22 pistol. He was fined $55 in the first incident and $50 in the second. Oswald had a security clearance in the Marines. There are four levels of security clearance—confidential, secret, top secret, and crypto. The unit to which Oswald was assigned was classified, and every man had to have a security clearance. The Warren Commission portrayed Oswald as having a confidential clearance, despite testimony contained in the Commission's own report that stated he had a higher clearance. There is strong evidence that suggests Oswald had a Crypto clearance, and to get a Crypto clearance one must pass a severe background check. Contrary to the Warren Commission's portrayal of him, Oswald was well liked in the Marines. His Marine friends considered him bright, quiet, serious, not a Marxist, and he never mentioned Communism for or against. Not one person thought Oswald had any gay tendencies. Everyone knew he was studying the Russian language, subscribed to a Russian-language newspaper, and had an interest in Russia. His pals jokingly called him "Comrade" and "Oswaldkovich." Oswald's buddies knew the reason listed for his discharge was false, and they were under the impression that Oswald was going to Switzerland to study. Despite the fact that the "official" reason for Oswald's discharge was hardship to take care of his mother, the Marine Corps was aware that this was not his intention and assisted him in getting his passport to go to Russia ten days before he was discharged.

David Ferrie, a resident of New Orleans, was arrested on November 25, 1963 for complicity in the assassination of President Kennedy. Ferrie was released without being charged. David Ferrie was a professional pilot, owned his own plane, and was a captain in the Civil Air Patrol when Oswald joined the Patrol in 1955. Ferrie's background included arrests on homosexual charges, and he was known to be critical of President Kennedy over Kennedy's handling of the Bay of Pigs. As to Kennedy's handling of the Bay of Pigs, Ferrie said that the President "ought to be shot." When the Garrison investigation indicated that David Ferrie was about to be arrested for complicity in the assassination of President Kennedy by Jim Garrison, Ferrie was found naked in his bed and dead. There were two suicide notes nearby. The coroner ruled his death was neither suicide nor murder, but natural. The day before Ferrie died, the Associated Press ran an article about Ferrie that stated, "Ferrie was in fear of his life." Ferrie had denied knowing Oswald to the Secret Service and the F.B.I.; however, in interviews with reporters, Ferrie made remarks to the press that would indicate that he did know Oswald and knew Oswald well. He made remarks such as, "my assessment of Oswald is that he would be incapable of any interpersonal relationship, especially anything as delicate as a conspiracy to kill."

David Ferrie was never called to testify before the Warren Commission, and there was no real investigation by the Commission on a Oswald-Ferrie connection. However, F.B.I. and Secret Service reports on Ferrie were directed to be sealed for 75 years.

After the death of her husband, the Secret Service and the F.B.I whisked Marina Oswald away to an Arlington, Texas hide-away and questioned her for hours. The transcript of that meeting shows that late in the questioning Marina was asked if she knew a man named Ferrie. The stenographer spelled it "Farry" in the transcript.

In the early 60's, there was a C.I.A.-sponsored Cuban refugee training camp near New Orleans on the shores of Lake Pontchartrain, southeast of Mandeville, Louisiana. This camp was a military camp with the sole purpose of training anti-Castro Cuban refugees for another invasion of Cuba, and was maintained and paid for by the Central Intelligence Agency. It was still active in the summer of 1963. Let me give some background as to why that camp was there. When Batista was overthrown in Cuba by Castro, President Eisenhower determined that Castro was a communist and something needed to be done about it. The C.I.A. was assigned this project and several million dollars was made available. An invasion was planned by "Cuban" refugees and the U.S. would give them air cover. Before the plan was put into operation, John F. Kennedy was elected President and took office. President Kennedy decided to let the C.I.A. go ahead with the invasion, and in mid-April 1961, the invasion began. The attack had no more than begun when President Kennedy received a wire from Russian Premier Nikita Khrushchev that said in part, "The whole world knows the United States government is behind the invasion of Cuba and the Soviet Union will defend Cuba if the invasion does not stop at once." The air cover that Kennedy had promised was called off and the 1,500 men in the invasion were either killed or captured and executed. The anti-Castro Cuban refugees have no love for President Kennedy. President Kennedy's speech in Miami on November 18, 1963, four days before he was assassinated, was also negative to the Cuban refugees. New Orleans had thousands of Cuban refugees living there in 1963 and few of them liked Kennedy.

New Orleans Attorney Dean Adams Andrews had the unique experience of being one of the only people subpoenaed by the Warren Commission. He was on Assistant Counsel Wesley J. Liebeler's list of people to depose on Liebeler's trip to New Orleans in April 1963, but was not deposed at that time. Andrews wanted to testify since he had information on the assassination, and he was belatedly called before the Commission on July 21, 1964. The subpoena requested that he bring with him anything and everything pertaining to Lee Harvey Oswald and any and all records of an attempt to hire Andrews by Clay Bertrand to represent Lee Harvey Oswald from April 1, 1963 through December 31, 1963. Clay

Bertrand was an alias for Clay Shaw whom New Orleans District Attorney Jim Garrison later charged with and put on trial for complicity in the assassination of President Kennedy. Words cannot describe Andrews; he was a flamboyant, jive-talking lawyer with his own slang, running for Parish Judge at the time of the assassination. Andrews was known to represent unpopular cases such as that of politicians and sex deviates. Assistant Counsel Wesley Liebeler took Andrews deposition and was armed with reports that the F.B.I. had made on interviews with Andrews. Andrews testified that Oswald came into his office three to five times, having gay kids with him one time and a Mexican another time. He said Oswald was asking about getting his discharge straightened out and American citizenship for his wife. When asked about what records he had brought with him, Andrews stated his office had been burglarized and he had none. Andrews also stated that Oswald was a patsy, no way he could have killed the President. Andrews testified that after the assassination he got a call from a man whose voice he recognized as Clay Bertrand's, requesting that he go to Dallas and defend Oswald. Andrews said he declined Bertrand's request, but did call fellow lawyer Sam Monk Zelden to see if Zelden would defend Oswald. When Andrews called Zelden, Zelden advised Andrews that Oswald had just died. Kept out of the Warren Report is an F.B.I. report made by Special Agents Kennedy and Schlaeger on November 25, 1963, of an interview with Sam Zelden that verifies Andrews statement that while they were discussing the possibility of defending Oswald, Zelden had his TV on and Zelden told Andrews that Oswald had been shot. Eva Springer, Andrews' secretary, confirmed that Andrews called her at home and discussed defending Oswald, and she said she was "not going to Dallas" with him and she wanted "nothing to do with the case." Andrews testified that Bertrand had called him before to get gay kids out of jail and that he thought it was Bertrand who sent Oswald in to see him. Liebeler tried to trip Andrews up with inconsistencies in his testimony and the Secret Service and F.B.I. reports on interviews with Andrews, but it did not faze Andrews. Not one of the Secret Service agents or F.B.I. agents that made the Andrews reports was called to testify and clear up any inconsistency. The truth is that there was no follow up or investigation by the Warren Commission of Andrews' claims about Clay Bertrand. It was late July and the Commission had planned to wind up its investigation by the end of June. In fact, the Commission had already begun to write their final report when the revelation that one shot had missed and hit the curb near me threw a kink in that plan. Two years after he testified before the Warren Commission, Dean Andrews recanted his story about Clay Bertrand, and in sworn testimony, Andrews said he lied to protect a client. Andrews was convicted of perjury and barred from practicing law. Why Andrews would suddenly say he lied to the Warren Commission, knowing it would cost him his law career, is a mystery.

Sylvia Odio belatedly testified before the Warren Commission on July 22, 1964. Ms. Odio was a Cuban refugee living in Dallas since March of 1963. Ms. Odio had previously gone to school for three years in Philadelphia at Eden Hall Convent of the Sacred Heart from 1951 to 1954, and had lived in New Orleans briefly in 1957. She first came to the U. S. to stay in 1960. Ms. Odio was studying law in Cuba when Castro took over and did not graduate from law school. She testified she was active in JURE (Juanta Revolutionary), which was headed by Monolo Ray, and helped the organization raise money. Ms. Odio stated that she and her sister Annie were watching TV after the President was assassinated, and when Oswald's picture appeared, they both recognized Oswald as a man that had been at their house a couple of months earlier. Ms. Odio said she was preparing to go out one evening when the doorbell rang. There were three people at the door; one seemed to be an American and the other two seemed to be Cuban. One of the men asked, "Are you Sarita Odio?" Sylvia Odio replied she was not, saying, "That is my sister studying at the University of Dallas; I am Sylvia." The man then asked, "Is she the oldest?" to which Sylvia Odio replied, "No, I am the oldest." The man then said, "It is you we are looking for." They introduced themselves as members of JURE and friends of her father, and Ms. Odio let them in. One of the Cubans introduced himself as Leopoldo, and Ms. Odio thought the other Cuban was something like Angelo. The American was introduced as Leon, and he was the man she later recognized as Lee Harvey Oswald on TV. The man named Leopoldo gave Ms. Odio incredible details about her father that few would know. Leopoldo finally said, "We want you to meet this American, he is Leon Oswald." He repeated it twice, and then said Leon was very much interested in the Cuban cause. Leopoldo then pulled out a letter written in Spanish about JURE and trying to raise money to overthrow Castro. Ms. Odio was asked to translate it into English so it could be sent out as an appeal for money to different industries. Ms. Odio asked if a couple of JURE members she knew in Dallas had sent them and they replied no, they had just come from New Orleans and were trying to get this organized. Ms. Odio told the men she did not have time to work on the letter and they left. The next evening Leopoldo called her and asked her what she thought about the American. Ms. Odio replied that she had not thought anything. Leopoldo went on to say the American is kind of nuts and, "he told us you Cubans don't have any guts, because President Kennedy should have been assassinated after the Bay of Pigs and some Cubans should have done that," and later, "It is so easy to do it." Ms. Odio's testimony covers over 20 pages in Volume XI. Wesley Liebeler was the assistant counsel taking her deposition and tries to compare what she is saying that day with what was in her F.B.I. interview on December 18, 1963. There are some minor differences, but nothing major as is normal when two statements are taken months apart. At the start of the deposition Ms. Odio states she does not know the date of meeting Leon Oswald, but Liebeler persists in trying to pin down the date and comes up with late September, a time when Lee Harvey Oswald was supposedly in Mexico. The Commission did ask the F.B.I to check out Ms. Odio's reputation for honesty; however, the final report was printed before the F.B.I. reported back on Ms. Odio's reputation for honesty. That her sister was there and recognized Oswald as well as her talking about it to a priest lends much credibility to Ms. Odio's testimony.

Carlos Bringuier fled Cuba with his wife and three children when Fidel Castro took over Cuba. In Cuba, Bringuier was a lawyer and a member of the Cuban Bar. Bringuier lived in New Orleans in 1963 and first met Lee Harvey Oswald in Bringuier's store on August 5, 1963. Bringuier was anti-Castro and a member of the Cuban Revolutionary Counsel and the Cuban Student Directorate in New Orleans. In that first meeting, Oswald and Bringuier talked for about an hour and a half, during which time Oswald showed a great interest in fighting Castro. Oswald stated he was against Castro and against Communism and asked Bringuier for some anti-Castro literature. Oswald told Bringuier that he was an ex-marine and that he would help train Cubans to fight Castro; he also said that he would fight Castro himself. As Oswald was about to leave the store, Oswald reached in his pocket and pulled out some money and offered to contribute to the anti-Castro cause. On August 6, 1963, Oswald returned to the store to give Carlos a copy of the Guidebook for Marines. On August 9, 1963, Bringuier discovered Oswald passing out pro-Castro literature on Canal Street. An argument ensued and Bringuier took off his glasses to hit Oswald. As Bringuier approached, Oswald dropped his hands and arms in front of him in an X, and said "hit me." The police arrived and arrested Oswald, Bringuier, and two of Bringuier's friends. At the Police Station Oswald asked to speak to an F.B.I. agent and one came to see Oswald. Bringuier and his friends had to post a $25 bond, but Oswald did not. On Monday, August 12, they all appeared in court, where Oswald plead guilty and paid a $10 fine. Bringuier and his friends plead not guilty, arguing their case to the Judge who found them not guilty. This minor incident led to a debate being sponsored by a local station between Oswald and Bringuier. Before the debate on August 16, Oswald and Bringuier shook hands. Bringuier was deposed by Wesley Liebeler on April 7-8 for the Warren Commission in New Orleans. His testimony is unique in that Liebeler lets Bringuier speak on any subject he wants, which is contrary to the control Liebeler exhibits in other depositions Liebeler took. In his testimony, Bringuier gives out many names of people active in both the anti-Castro and pro-Castro movements, but little of the information given by Bringuier was followed up on by the Warren Commission.

It took years for researchers to discover the real problem the Warren Commission had in investigating Oswald in New Orleans. New Orleans was a hotbed for C.I.A. activities in relation to the

Cuban situation. The full truth will never be known. What is known was that the C.I.A. was running illegal military training camps for Cuban refugees, had informants, had shady characters involved, illegal money movements, illegal arms movements, and had a plan in motion to have Castro assassinated (that became public later). An investigation into Lee Harvey Oswald in New Orleans could blow the lid off the C.I.A.'s covers. The F.B.I. and the Secret Service were aware of the C.I.A.'s operations. The Cuban refugees hated Castro and there was no love lost for President Kennedy because he had reneged on his promise of help with the Bay of Pigs fiasco, costing the lives of hundreds of anti-Castro Cubans. When Assistant Warren Commission Counsel Wesley J. Liebeler went to New Orleans to take depositions from witnesses, he was tipped off and cautioned about who he should talk to. One of the Cubans Liebeler did not want to talk to was Orest Pena. Liebeler was forced to take Pena's testimony and finally did belatedly on July 21, 1964. Orest Pena's testimony can be found in volume XI, page 346 to 364. Mr. Pena was born in Cuba and in 1956 became an American citizen. Orest Pena owned Habana Bar and Lounge in New Orleans at 117 Decatur Street. He was an F.B.I. informant, belonged to a couple of anti-Castro organizations in New Orleans, had known David Ferrie for several years, saw Oswald in his bar at one time with two Mexicans (or Cubans), knew Carlos Bringuier, knew Sergio Arcacha Smith, and the list went on and on with people connected with the Cuban underground. When Arcacha's name was mentioned by Pena, Liebeler changed the subject. When Pena wanted to talk about certain things, Liebeler would say, "We can come back to that later." Pena had been interviewed over and over by the F.B.I. and other Federal Agencies before and after the assassination. Liebeler pretended to know of only two F.B.I. reports of interviews with Pena while Pena stated there were 15 or 20. In the summer of 1963, Pena traveled to Mexico, Puerto Rico, the Dominican Republic, London, Paris, Madrid, Rome, Berlin, and Communist-controlled East Berlin. All, he said, while on vacation. There was not a serious Warren Commission investigation of Oswald's connections in New Orleans. New Orleans District Attorney Jim Garrison was secretly investigating New Orleans connections to the assassination when it was leaked to the press on Friday, February 18, 1967 that an investigation into the assassination of President Kennedy was in progress by his office. One of the main characters Garrison was investigating was David Ferrie. On March 31, 1967, Clay Shaw was arrested in New Orleans by Jim Garrison for conspiracy to assassinate President Kennedy. Garrison stated that Clay Shaw was also Clay Bertrand. Clay Shaw was a wealthy businessman who had managed the International Trade Mart in New Orleans. The arrest came as a shock to New Orleans society because Shaw was a well-respected bachelor active in high society life. With the release of this news, different statements came from the Justice Department and former Warren Commission members. Ramsey Clark, now the United States Attorney General, said, "On the evidence the F.B.I. has, there was no connection found between Shaw and the assassination of President Kennedy on November 22, 1963." There is a big problem with Clark's statement, however, since nowhere in the thousands of pages in the 26 volumes is Clay Shaw mentioned or investigated in any way. To further contradict Clark's statement, Warren Commission General Counsel J. Lee Rankin said, "I have never heard of any Clay Shaw." Another Justice Department official, in referring to Clark's statement said, "Clay Shaw and Clay Bertrand are one and the same; it's the same guy." The Warren Commission never found anyone named Bertrand to investigate, and the only place the name Bertrand appears is in Dean Andrews' testimony. Now we have a man that the Warren Commission never heard of cleared by the F.B.I. in the President's assassination and a man the Commission could not find also cleared by the F.B.I. in the assassination. How did the F.B.I. investigate a man they never heard of and another man they could not find? Or did in fact the F.B.I. investigate Bertrand, found out he was Clay Shaw, investigated Shaw and then never told the Warren Commission? To the contrary, there is one reference in the report stating, "investigation has failed to locate the person (Bertrand) who supposedly called Andrews." With the negative comments coming from the United States Department of Justice, the press was skeptical and belittled Garrison's efforts.

A search warrant was requested and granted for a search of Clay Shaw's home, with the reason given for the search Warrant being that in September 1963 there was a meeting at David Ferrie's apartment between David Ferrie, Clay Shaw (alias Clay Bertrand), Lee Harvey Oswald, and an informant and other persons, and that at this meeting the above named individuals were discussing how they would kill John F. Kennedy, President of the United States. Further, a confidential informant was present at this meeting and saw and heard David Ferrie, Clay Shaw (alias Clay Bertrand), and Lee Harvey Oswald agree to kill John F. Kennedy and discuss the means and manner of carrying out this agreement. The affidavit went on to say that the confidential informant had come forward voluntarily and had been administered sodium pentothal (truth serum) under the care and control and supervision of the coroner for the Parish of New Orleans, a medical doctor. The confidential informant verified, corroborated, and reaffirmed his earlier statements while under the sodium pentothal. Shaw's luxurious home was searched for three hours by twelve of Garrison's agents and they left carrying five boxes of items, including a shotgun or rifle (Shaw had maintained he would not allow a gun in his home), an Army cartridge belt, five whips, a black hood and cape, journals, a book entitled "A Holiday for Murder," rope, a chain, pieces of chain, pieces of leather, a black net hat, and a black gown. The articles seemed to verify what Dean Andrews had said, "that Bertrand was a swinging cat." Most single men do not have an affinity for dresses, chains, and whips.

In New Orleans, Jim Garrison had the reputation of taking on the impossible and winning, which included fights with the Mayor and judges. His battles with judges that he lost at the local level he won on appeal to the State Supreme Court. Garrison went against the normal for Shaw, asking for a preliminary hearing to obtain a judicial determination of whether there were grounds to bring Shaw to trial. The case was in Criminal District Court Judge Bernard J. Begert's court. Judge Begert appointed two other judges, Malcolm V. O'Hara and Mathew S. Braniff, to serve with him. All three would hear the case and decisions would be made by majority vote. Judge Begert announced strong rules for the courtroom, such as no picture taking, no witness statements outside the court room, admission to the courtroom of accredited representatives only, and a search of all those entering the courtroom. The press was having a field day throwing arrows at Garrison. It had been just a little over two years since the Warren Commission had published its findings, and the American public had accepted those findings (at the time) as the truth, including me.

Perry Raymond Russo was the confidential informant. Russo was a college student and sold insurance part time to pay his was through school. His neighbors and friends all spoke highly of Russo. Russo testified that he had met David Ferrie while in the Civil Air Patrol, becoming friends with Ferrie, and that he had been in Ferrie's apartment 30 to 40 times. Russo testified that Clay Shaw (alias Clay Bertrand), David Ferrie, Lee Harvey Oswald, and others were at Ferrie's apartment sometime in October of 1963 when plans were agreed on to kill President Kennedy. Oswald had been introduced as Leon Oswald; Shaw had been introduced as "Clem" Bertrand. The defense tried to trip Russo up over the fact that at one time he did not recognize Oswald. Russo explained that when he saw Oswald at Ferrie's apartment, he was unshaven and dirty looking, but the pictures he had seen of Oswald on TV showed Oswald clean-shaven and somewhat neat. The Prosecution produced a picture of Oswald they had had an artist draw with beard stubble, which Russo used to identify Oswald. The Defense tried to introduce the 26 volumes of the Warren Report in their defense, but it was denied as hearsay. Vernon Bundy, a reforming dope user, also took the stand and testified he saw Shaw and Oswald together and saw Shaw give Oswald a roll of money. The three judges found that there was enough evidence for Clay Shaw to go to trial for conspiracy to murder the President.

From the time of the preliminary hearing until Clay Shaw stood trial, Jim Garrison was belittled by the press, had no cooperation from federal agencies, and the negative publicity caused major problems with potential witnesses, some of them fleeing the state to avoid testifying. The result was that Garrison did not present a good case against Clay Shaw and Shaw was found not guilty by a jury two years after being arrested. At the time Clay Shaw was found not guilty by a jury in New Orleans, most F.B.I. documents concerning the assassination of President Kennedy had been sealed from the public for 75 years. Clay Shaw may have been innocent of a conspiracy to assassinate President Kennedy, but his known association with certain elements of New Orleans society should have been investigated by the Warren Commission to determine what Oswald's connection to the Cuban refugees was or wasn't. What we have learned from these now released documents is that there was an interlaced web of intrigue concerning anti-Castro Cuban refugees, pro-Castro Cuban refugees, C.I.A. involvement, F.B.I. involvement, stolen arms, money, and the aforementioned individuals and others, all in the interest of removing Castro from power in Cuba. There is no question that there was a secret C.I.A. plot to remove a foreign head of state from power, Fidel Castro of Cuba. The question is still open to this day whether someone in this group of Cuban refugees also conspired to assassinate President Kennedy. We were to learn years later, when it became public knowledge, that even the Mafia was contacted by a U.S, Government agency to assassinate Fidel Castro. To what degree Assistant Warren Commission Counsel Wesley J. Liebeler knew of C.I.A. and F.B.I. involvement with these refugees is unknown. Someone must have put a bug in his ear not to pry, that there were too many individuals with connections to the aforementioned and Lee Harvey Oswald. Too many people with too much information were not called to testify. With the few who were called to testify, Commission Counsel Liebeler changed the subject when it seemed like they were going to say something about the secret C.I.A., F.B.I., and Cuban activities in New Orleans.

Lee Harvey Oswald used the return address of 544 Camp Street on his pro-Castro Fair Play for Cuba literature. This location was the headquarters for an anti-Castro group, the Cuban Revolutionary Council. The building at 544 Camp Street was on the corner of Camp and Lafayette streets. Guy Banister and Associates Inc., a private detective agency, was in the same building, but used Lafayette Street as their address. Guy Banister was a former F.B.I. Agent and was active in anti-Castro causes before and after the Bay of Pigs fiasco, and Bannister had C.I.A. connections. David Ferrie met with Cubans in Banister's office, Lee Harvey Oswald was seen in Banister's office with Cubans, and the list of connections to Guy Bannister and anti-Castro activities in New Orleans goes on and on. When Banister's secretary placed Oswald in Banister's office, she was promptly discredited as an unreliable witness. When one's character is attacked by the C.I.A. or F.B.I., it usually shuts them up and changes their testimony. There is more than ample evidence that the C.I.A. used Guy Banister as a go-between to the anti-Castro Cubans. There is equally ample evidence that there was a plot to overthrow or assassinate Fidel Castro. There is also evidence that some of these anti-Castro Cubans hated President Kennedy for backing out of the Bay of Pigs. Finally, there is plenty of evidence that Lee Harvey Oswald was involved with the anti-Castro Cubans and the anti-Castro Cubans were involved with the C.I.A. What we do know is that we will never know what this mountain of evidence would have led to. I do not believe in any way shape or form that the C.I.A. had anything to do with the assassination of President John F. Kennedy. I do have personal knowledge, however, that leads me to believe that there was an Oswald-C.I.A. link that was covered up, in the interest of national security.

I have included on the following 3 pages, a copy of an internal F.B.I. memorandum made 2 and ½ years after the assassination of President Kennedy between two top F.B.I. officials, Tolson and DeLoach, about an interview DeLoach had with famed Pulitzer Prize winning reporter Jack Anderson. Jack Anderson was the syndicated Columnist, who in 1972, exposed the C.I.A.'s plot to assassinate Fidel Castro. This internal F.B.I. memorandum is revealing in its content.

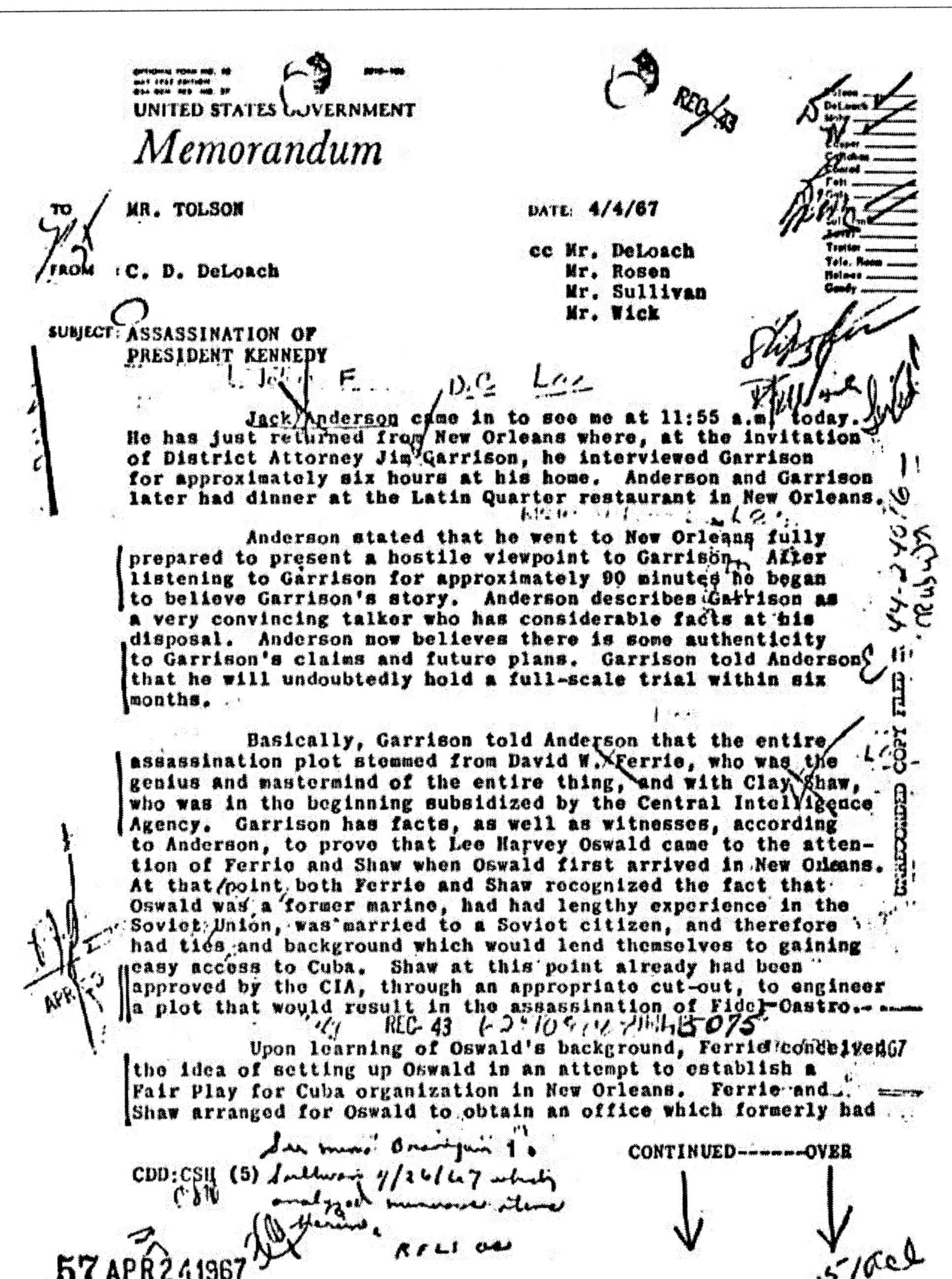

UNITED STATES GOVERNMENT

Memorandum

TO : MR. TOLSON

DATE: 4/4/67

FROM : C. D. DeLoach

cc Mr. DeLoach
Mr. Rosen
Mr. Sullivan
Mr. Wick

SUBJECT: ASSASSINATION OF PRESIDENT KENNEDY

Jack Anderson came in to see me at 11:55 a.m. today. He has just returned from New Orleans where, at the invitation of District Attorney Jim Garrison, he interviewed Garrison for approximately six hours at his home. Anderson and Garrison later had dinner at the Latin Quarter restaurant in New Orleans.

Anderson stated that he went to New Orleans fully prepared to present a hostile viewpoint to Garrison. After listening to Garrison for approximately 90 minutes he began to believe Garrison's story. Anderson describes Garrison as a very convincing talker who has considerable facts at his disposal. Anderson now believes there is some authenticity to Garrison's claims and future plans. Garrison told Anderson that he will undoubtedly hold a full-scale trial within six months.

Basically, Garrison told Anderson that the entire assassination plot stemmed from David W. Ferrie, who was the genius and mastermind of the entire thing, and with Clay Shaw, who was in the beginning subsidized by the Central Intelligence Agency. Garrison has facts, as well as witnesses, according to Anderson, to prove that Lee Harvey Oswald came to the attention of Ferrie and Shaw when Oswald first arrived in New Orleans. At that point both Ferrie and Shaw recognized the fact that Oswald was a former marine, had had lengthy experience in the Soviet Union, was married to a Soviet citizen, and therefore had ties and background which would lend themselves to gaining easy access to Cuba. Shaw at this point already had been approved by the CIA, through an appropriate cut-out, to engineer a plot that would result in the assassination of Fidel Castro.

REC-43

Upon learning of Oswald's background, Ferrie conceived the idea of setting up Oswald in an attempt to establish a Fair Play for Cuba organization in New Orleans. Ferrie and Shaw arranged for Oswald to obtain an office which formerly had

CDD:CSH (5)

CONTINUED------OVER

57 APR 24 1967

Mr. Tolson

been rented by an anti-Castro organization. Ferrie and Shaw also conceived the idea of sending Oswald to Mexico in a fake attempt to obtain permission to re-enter the Soviet Union. Garrison, according to Anderson, can prove that Oswald did this merely to establish a good atmosphere so that he could gain ready access to Cuba.

Garrison claims that it was at this point that Oswald became disillusioned and refused to go through with the plot to assassinate Castro. Upon returning to New Orleans from Mexico, Oswald advised both Ferrie and Shaw that he would not go through with their plans. Shaw and Ferrie, being guided by several Cubans in their midst, then conceived the idea (mostly because of the fiasco at the Bay of Pigs) of assassinating President Kennedy. Ferrie and Shaw believed that Oswald could be the "patsy" and instructed him to go to Dallas for the purpose of the assassination.

They also engineered the idea of him buying the gun under the name of A. J. Hidell, and the use of the mails in procuring this gun so that it would be an open, public record which could be traced to Oswald. They additionally told Oswald that he should keep certain papers in his possession which would trace back to the gun.

On the day of the assassination, Ferrie traveled to Houston, allegedly for the purpose of ice skating. Witnesses at the ice skating rink remember Ferrie as being at the rink and have indicated to Garrison that Ferrie, while he did not ice skate, did stand near a pay telephone at all times on the day of 11/22/63.

Garrison also has witnesses who will testify that Jack Ruby was the eyes and ears for Ferrie at all times. Ruby sent two of his people to Houston so that, upon the success of the assassination attempt, these two people could use a local pay phone to advise Ferrie of the success of the plot. Garrison claims that a long distance phone call from Dallas to Houston could, of course, have been traced; hence the desirability of using the local phone. Anderson stated that Ruby was definitely in on the plot and was later instructed by Ferrie and Shaw to take care of Oswald.

2

Mr. Tolson

Anderson next sprang the "Sixty-four dollar question." He stated that at the close of Garrison's six-hour recitation of facts, he (Anderson) was of the opinion that Garrison was not only sincere, but very convincing. Anderson stated that Garrison firmly believed his facts. Anderson then told me that he bluntly asked Garrison why Garrison had not given all these convincing facts to the FBI, whereupon Garrison replied, "I got started off on the wrong foot with the FBI." Garrison added, "I would be more than willing to give the FBI everything I have and let them finish the investigation if they so desire."

Anderson told me that he, of course, is now in a position to contact Garrison and indicate that the FBI will or will not take over this case. I told Anderson that the FBI would not under any circumstances take over the case. I stated that Garrison had made it quite plain that he did not want the cooperation of the FBI and, as a matter of fact, Garrison had threatened to put handcuffs on any of our agents who approached him for information.

I also told Anderson that, while we of course would accept any information that was voluntarily given to us, we at the same time would not take over Garrison's "dirty laundry."

Anderson told me that if the Bureau had any change of policy in the above regard he would appreciate knowing about it. I told him we would keep his offer in mind; however, there definitely would be no change of policy.

Anderson also told me that he had discussed this entire matter with George Christian, the President's Press Secretary, at the White House. He stated that Christian was also convinced that there must be some truth to Garrison's allegations. Christian told Anderson to get in touch with the FBI. Anderson stated he had already been planning to do this, but that he now especially wanted to advise us of the full facts because of Christian's request. Lyndon B. Johnson

In this connection, Marvin Watson called me late last night and stated that the President had told him, in an off moment, that he was now convinced that there was a plot in connection with the assassination. Watson stated the President felt that CIA had had something to do with this plot. Watson requested that any further information we could furnish

Central Intelligence Agency

3

over

POST MORTEM

Post Mortem, what an apt name for my final chapter; it was the name of one of the books written by my dear friend and mentor Harold Weisberg on the assassination of President Kennedy. The book is hard to read, but is one of the best-researched and most factual books written on the assassination. Unfortunately, the book has been out of print since 1975, but if you can find a copy, I recommend it for anyone wanting to learn more about the assassination than what I have written here. J. Edgar Hoover detested Harold and had standing orders for no one in the F.B.I. to cooperate with Harold. However, other F.B.I. officials have stated publicly that Harold Weisberg was the most knowledgeable person in America on the assassination of President Kennedy. Harold stayed after me for years to write this book, and I am sorry he will not be here to comment on it. Harold died in 2002.

The man named to head up the HEARINGS BEFORE THE PRESIDENT'S COMMISSION ON THE ASSASSINATION OF PRESIDENT KENNEDY was United States Supreme Court Chief Justice Earl Warren. Chief Justice Warren and I agree on one thing, "We will never know what really happened in Dallas that day." Then and now this Commission was and is best known as the Warren Commission, seven men selected by President Lyndon Johnson to be a blue ribbon committee to conduct hearings on the death of President John F. Kennedy in Dallas, Texas on November 22, 1963. These seven men knew when they signed their final report that questions remained unanswered about what really happened in Dallas that fateful day. Critics have had 40 years to pore over that final report and tear it apart, and the critics have done just that. Three of these seven men did not want to sign the final report. These three did sign the final report with reservations after words such as "possible" and "probable" were used. A fourth member, Earl Warren, made the statement I quoted above. A fifth member, Representative Gerald Ford, acted as the eyes and ears of the Commission for J. Edgar Hoover. The Commission meetings and all discussions held by these seven members were supposed to be held in secret. Unknown to the other six members, however, Representative Ford was reporting to F.B.I. Director J. Edgar Hoover everything these seven men discussed in these secret meetings. The seven Warren Commission members did not sit in on most of the hearings. They only sat in if they felt if it was someone of importance, like Mrs. Kennedy, Governor Connally, the Parkland doctors, or the autopsy doctors. In most of the hearings that Commission members did attend, not all seven members would be present. There were times too that when a Commission member did attend, he would excuse himself and leave in the middle of testimony. Ordinary witnesses like me were questioned by one of the 14 staff lawyers, usually with just that lawyer, a stenographer, and the witness present. The staff lawyers had a preset list of questions to ask the witnesses, and if a witness started to volunteer information other than what was on the staff lawyer's list of questions, the staff lawyer would often change the subject. These 14 staff lawyers did the questioning of the witnesses and then reported their interpretation of the witness's answers to the Commission members. There was no balance. In the hearings, the taking of a deposition by a staff lawyer held to one line of pre-determined questioning, disallowing any inquiries to the contrary. Such a rigid approach failed to bring out the more in-depth information needed from the witness. The Warren Commission, including the 14 staff lawyers did not have one investigator on their staff, none. All investigations were done by the Secret Service, the C.I.A., and the F.B.I., with the F.B.I. doing most of them.

To the seven Commission members' credit, they recognized that they were going to have a problem with getting J. Edgar Hoover and the F.B.I.'s cooperation and discussed that fact in one of their early meetings. Hoover had grown too big for his britches and the Warren Commission knew it. In fact, Hoover's ego and feeling of self-importance had grown so big that when Hoover testified before the Commission, Hoover referred to his F.B.I. as "the seat of Government." Unknown to the Commission and before the Commission was even named, Hoover had sent secret internal F.B.I. memos to his department heads. In one memo, written just two days after the assassination, he said, "Bureau must convince public Oswald is the real assassin." In just another four days after the assassination, one memo said, "Wrap up investigation, seems to me we have the basic facts now." And in another memo issued seven days after the assassination, his words were, "Hope to have investigation wrapped up by next week." Then, when the Warren Commission was named, Hoover instructed F.B.I. agents not to volunteer information to the Commission. Hoover also ordered that no Bureau official attend the early

Warren Commission sessions. Later, Hoover pledged openly, "Case will remain open for all time," but internally Hoover designated, "Case closed in internal Bureau files." The Warren Commission, named to have hearings to find the truth about the assassination of President John F. Kennedy, was doomed from the start.

One cannot escape the fact that Lee Harvey Oswald was in some way involved in the assassination of President Kennedy to some degree; there is too much evidence to support that conclusion. Oswald could have fired the three shots that we all heard that day or he could have been set up as a patsy, which many qualified researchers have claimed. One thing is certain; we will never be sure of what his real involvement was in the assassination.

I heard three shots that day, and almost every other witness heard three shots. A couple of witnesses thought they heard four shots, and a couple more witnesses thought they heard five or six shots. There were three shots and only three shots that were "heard" that day in Dealey Plaza, and 98% of the known 250 plus witnesses heard three shots. In the previous chapters, I used only the three shots that I heard to base my conclusions on the sequence of the shots. There is just as much, if not more, evidence that there were more than three shots fired in Dealey Plaza, and maybe even as many as three shooters. More than three shots would have meant there was a conspiracy to kill President Kennedy. For reasons we will never know, J. Edgar Hoover and other higher-ups in Washington made a snap decision within hours of the assassination that there would be no finding of a conspiracy; Oswald was to be a lone nut assassin. That Oswald fired off three shots in five and a half seconds with the rifle found in the Schoolbook Depository is hogwash. The Warren Commission could not find one ace marksman to duplicate that feat. In the 40 years since the assassination, not one person has been able to fire, reload, aim, and get off three shots with a rifle such as the one found in the Schoolbook Depository in five and one half seconds. That President Kennedy and Governor Connally were hit by one bullet is more hogwash. That a bullet could pass through the bodies of two men, shatter a rib and wrist bones and remain in pristine condition, such as Commission Exhibit No. 399, is hogwash. Every effort by the Warren Commission to duplicate this feat failed. Further, that a downward moving bullet could hit the President six inches below the collar line in his back and then suddenly change directions and go up to exit his throat, and then jump sideways and go down again to hit Governor Connally, is more hogwash. That an object (the President's head) hit by a bullet traveling at 2,000 feet per second would violently react toward the source of that bullet is more hogwash. A man, or an animal for that matter, are blown away from the source of the shot. THERE WERE MORE THAN THREE SHOTS FIRED AT PRESIDENT KENNEDY AND GOVERNOR CONNALLY THAT DAY. When one accepts this simple fact, that there was more than one shooter, at least one or maybe more, equipped with a silencer and firing at the President, the answers to all of the injuries to both men and a shot that missed become easy. With more than three shots fired, the possible ways to explain these men's injuries are endless.

I do not want to speculate, but I will outline one possible scenario for thought, and just for thought only, that would answer some of the unanswered questions. The autopsy doctors found an entrance wound in the President's back about six inches below the collar line. The doctors could only probe this wound about an inch and it had a downward path of 45 to 60 degrees. With just these two known facts, a much earlier shot than thought by the Commission was made soon after the limousine turned on to Elm Street. The shot was fired from high up and sooner to get the 45 to 60 degree downward angle. It was a dud though, making a pop like a firecracker (that's what we all heard on the first shot), only penetrating the President's back an inch (that's what the autopsy doctors found). This dud bullet, still in pristine condition, then worked its way out of the President's back while he was being attended to at Parkland Hospital. The bullet was later found on the floor at Parkland Hospital and is now Commission Exhibit No. 399.

In the Zapruder movie, it shows the President emerging from behind the traffic sign seemingly reaching for his throat. What if the President is not reaching for a throat injury, but is only reacting to being hit in the back by a bullet? Test this on a friend, without your friend knowing what you are going to do. Sharply poke him in the back, and watch as your friend's arms come up exactly as President Kennedy's did after being hit in the back by a dud bullet. It is a natural reaction to a sharp poke or bullet to the back. Governor Connally is then hit by a shot aimed at the President; the shot misses the President and hits the Governor. The President is then hit in the head at almost the same instant by two separate shots, a shot from the rear and a shot from the right front (the grassy knoll). The Zapruder movie captures a slight forward movement of the head an inch or two as the bullet from the rear hits the President a split second before the bullet from the front hits the President. The shot from the grassy knoll blew the President's head back so violently that the momentum and energy from the backward head movement also threw the President's shoulders violently back and to the left and into the back of the seat. The right side and rear of his head is blown out as the Parkland doctors and nurses observed. Blood and brain tissue bathed everyone in the limousine. The motorcycle policeman riding at the left rear of the limousine was covered with blood and brain tissue, and pieces of the President's skull flew out of the vehicle. One large piece of skull from the rear of the President's head was found lying in the street by the curb an hour later. A small fragment from the rear headshot exited the President's throat making the small throat wound that the Parkland doctors and nurses observed. As the Presidential limousine approaches the triple underpass, Mrs. Kennedy crawls onto the trunk of the limousine to retrieve a piece of the President's skull, and a Secret Service agent runs from the follow up car and pushes Mrs. Kennedy back into the seat. As Mrs. Kennedy was being pushed back into the seat, a final random missed shot sailed high over the limousine and hit the curb near where I was standing, sending flying debris into my face. The witnesses on the grassy knoll all said that at least one shot came from behind them and one witness, a soldier in uniform, swears one shot whizzed by his ear. Senator Ralph Yarborough, who was riding in the motorcade, saw this soldier throw himself to ground and thought at the time, "that soldier has experienced gunfire." Six of the railroad men standing on the overpass saw a puff of smoke come from the trees behind the grassy knoll during the shooting.

This scenario is just for thought because we will never know exactly what happened that day, November 22, 1963, in Dallas. I do know that by my being there as a witness, having a close association with the most recognized expert on the assassination, Harold Weisberg, and doing a 40-year study of the available evidence that there were in fact more shots fired than the three shots that we witnesses heard.

Through the years, there have been claims of a cover-up by many critics of the Warren Commission. There were cover-ups, but not on the grand scale that some of these critics would want us to believe. The cover-ups were small, compared to the overall picture and they were in the nature of CYA, cover your —. One such cover-up was that of Jack Ruby by the F.B.I. Jack Ruby acting alone and on impulse killed accused assassin Lee Harvey Oswald two days after the assassination. The problem that created for J. Edgar Hoover was that Jack Ruby was a paid informant for the F.B.I., and J. Edgar Hoover could not let that become public at all cost as the press and the public might think the F.B.I. was involved in a conspiracy to kill the President. The F.B.I was not involved in any conspiracy to kill the President in any way shape or form, but Hoover knew that at the very least a Ruby connection would have given the F.B.I. a black eye. Jack Ruby was accidentally at the right place at the right time, period, and he thought he would be a hero for killing Oswald. Ruby acted on an impulse that had nothing to do with any connection Ruby had with the F.B.I. Jack Ruby acted alone and was not a part of any plot. Another cover-up is a little more complicated and that was Lee Harvey Oswald's connection to the C.I.A. The C.I.A. had nothing to do with the assassination of President Kennedy, but the C.I.A. had a similar problem to the F.B.I. Oswald had done some undercover work for the C.I.A. Though not a C.I.A. agent, there is credible evidence that there were Oswald/C.I.A. connections in New Orleans with the Cuban situation that had to be covered up. There is credible evidence that Oswald's going to Russia had an Oswald/C.I.A. connection. What the exact details of these connections were, I do not know. I do know, because I heard it with my own ears, what an American Doctor said about knowing Oswald in Russia while the doctor and Oswald were both in Russia. The doctor, while undergoing persistent questions about knowing Oswald in Russia, finally said, "Well, I guess it is all out in the open now; it was a C.I.A. operation." The C.I.A. had nothing to do with the assassination of President Kennedy, but for the public to find out that the man charged with the assassination of a President had once done some undercover work for the C.I.A. would have been a disaster for the C.I.A. It had to be covered up. These two small cover-ups that I have just cited are understandable as it is part of human nature to CYA. There were probably other small cover-ups that we will never know about, but there is no evidence that any Federal, State, or local agency was involved in any cover-up concerning a plot to assassinate President Kennedy.

Withholding of evidence and tampering with evidence is another matter, however. I have had firsthand experience with the F.B.I. withholding and tampering with evidence. That one shot missed the President's limousine and hit the curb near me was not a secret. Seven minutes after the assassination, a motorcycle policeman radioed in about the shot and it was recorded on tape. Deputy Sheriff Buddy Walters was the first to spot the scar on the curb a minute or two after the shooting and led several of his fellow deputies to the scar. Homicide Detective Gus Rose took my statement in the Dallas Police Homicide office that very afternoon. Several witnesses saw the bullet hit the curb; one was a Dallas Police Officer who led the Dallas Police Crime Lab to the spot. Photographers took pictures of the scar. Two F.B.I. agents interviewed me and took a statement about the missed shot. Yet, when J. Edgar Hoover made his report to President Johnson and the Warren Commission, there was no mention of a missed shot. There is the probability that if the Jim Lehrer article about me had not appeared in the DALLAS TIMES HERALD on June 5, 1964, the final Warren report would have said there were three shots, that the first hit Kennedy, the second hit Connally, and the third hit the President in the head. There also would have been no mention of the missed shot. The Lehrer article caught the attention of the Warren Commission. In July, 1964, when Warren Commission General Counsel J. Lee Rankin asked Hoover to locate the mark on the curb, Hoover was still not ready to concede to the Commission that one shot went wild and hit the curb. Hoover reported back to Rankin that there was no mark to be found. Rankin did not give up, and with pictures taken of the curb shortly after the assassination, Rankin told Hoover to go back and have his agents find the mark. Eight months after the assassination of President John F. Kennedy, the F.B.I. located the mark on the curb. It was still in the same place as on November 22, 1963 and the point of impact where the bullet hit was still visible. On August 5, eight and one half months after the assassination, the curb was cut out of the street and sent to the F.B.I. laboratory for spectrographic analysis. Lead and traces of antimony were found, but no copper, which led Hoover to state it was a fragment that hit the curb. The Warren Commission dismissed Hoover's statement about no copper found and decided it was indeed a missed shot, and not a fragment that hit the curb. The curb section is in the National Archives. Ballistic evidence about the curb has been a source of controversy. A Federal lawsuit was filed to have an independent examination of the F.B.I.'s spectrographic analysis of the curb mark. The lawsuit drug on for years with the F.B.I. lawyers fighting every inch of the way to keep the spectrographic analysis film from being examined by an independent expert. The lawsuit ended after years of litigation with a statement by F.B.I. lawyers that this wafer thin piece of evidence had been thrown away to make room for storage. I have personally examined the mark on the curb in the National Archives with an assistant manager of the Archives, and we both agreed without hesitation, that the mark has been patched by a mortar-like substance. I also have a copy of an engineering report that was requested by a respected major U.S. monthly magazine in 1983. The report says the scar on the curb had been patched. I also have a photograph taken by F.B.I. Agent Shaneyfelt on August 5, 1963, the day the curb was cut out of the street and just prior to the curb being cut out of the street, that shows the curb had been patched before it was removed. Someone did not want known the fact that one shot went wild and missed the President's limousine, and it does not take a rocket scientist to figure out who that was. The curb is in the National Archives, and if it has not been re-tampered with, it is proof of another cover-up.

The doctors and nurses who were the first to see the President's injuries at Parkland Hospital observed a large part of the back of the Presidents skull blown out. The rewritten autopsy report (the original was deliberately burned by Dr. Humes) did not show the same injury to the back of the President's head. When the Parkland doctors were called to testify, they were told what questions they would be asked and shown the "official" autopsy report before they testified. This prepping of the Parkland doctors before testifying raises questions. The prepping had to have an influence on some of the doctors' testimonies. It did not apparently influence some of the doctors though and those doctors raised more questions about the integrity of the autopsy and the Warren Report. When the House of Representatives reopened the investigation in 1978, the President's autopsy photographs and x-rays were finally made available to the Parkland doctors and those in attendance at the autopsy. Many said some of the photographs and x-rays were not what they remembered seeing, and at least one autopsy technician said some were phonies. The House of Representatives committee's re-investigation was just as controversial, if not more so, than the Warren Report. The House Committee did determine that there was a conspiracy to assassinate President Kennedy.

In fact, there is more than a good probability that there was a conspiracy to assassinate President Kennedy. There is strong evidence that this conspiracy originated in New Orleans with disgruntled Cuban refugees and others over Kennedy's handling of the Bay of Pigs. The ones involved in the conspiracy had C.I.A. connections, such as participating in fake burglaries of military arms and ammunition for C.I.A.-sponsored anti-Castro activities to rid Cuba of Fidel Castro. If someone was caught with these arms, the government could then say the arms were stolen, and not given to these anti-Castro fighters by the U.S. Government. The C.I.A. was not involved and was totally unaware of any plot to kill the President. These men were acting on their own and the C.I.A. was not any part of any plot. New Orleans District Attorney Jim Garrison had some underground information about the plot to assassinate President Kennedy, but lacked enough information to prosecute and make a case. Garrison did try to make a case, but the action was ill-timed. Assistant Warren Commission Counsel Wesley J. Liebeler's lack of asking for depositions from key New Orleans individuals raises questions. There simply was not a reasonable inquiry by the Warren Commission into the New Orleans connections, and we will never know the truth about the New Orleans connections to the assassination

There are many personal lessons I have learned from this experience. One lesson is about eyewitness testimony. Witnesses standing side by side sometimes do not see the same thing, no matter how well-meaning they may be. Witnesses might change their testimony and others might enhance their testimony for their own purposes. Witnesses are often influenced by what they read in the newspaper and see on television. I know because there were a couple of times I was almost influenced by what I had read or saw on television. I had to back off and remind myself that I could only speak of what I actually witnessed, no more, no less, and that I could not let some outside influence alter what I knew as fact. Another lesson was that a newspaper article or television report was just one person's and his editor's interpretation of that event, that their interpretation was not always right, or that they might have a bias to the actual facts they are reporting for their own gain. Another lesson was that when you tell someone the truth as you know the truth to be, people will sometimes change what you have said for their own personal gain. Another lesson is the effect that the one in power can have on those under him. We have all seen it, when the one in power tells a person to do something, even if it is wrong, that person will do the wrong if he wants to keep his job. Another lesson, and probably the most important one, was about people. I learned that no matter what position one holds in life, whether it be a politician, an F.B.I. agent, a priest/preacher, a cop on the street, or the people you work with, there are decent god-fearing people who do right and there are a few bad apples. In this book, I have found fault with F.B.I. Director J. Edgar Hoover and he deserves it. If one man could be blamed for the controversy over the Warren Report, it would be Hoover. We will never know how much crucial information Hoover withheld from the Warren Commission. By all accounts, Hoover at one time was an asset to our country, but by 1963 his ego was out of control and the mess the F.B.I. was in for years after Hoover can be traced back to Hoover. Waco, Ruby Ridge, and the non-handling of pre-9/11 information are examples. In spite of there being a few bad apples in every profession, however, the good people far exceed the bad apples, and that applies to the Federal Bureau of Investigation as well. Some of the best men and women this country has ever known were and are F.B.I. agents. My criticism of the F.B.I. is not aimed at these hard working, smart, brave, and honest F.B.I. agents. If I have offended one of these good agents, I apologize; my criticism was not aimed at you. I have just touched on some of the high points of the assassination of President Kennedy and the Warren Commission's Hearings. There are hundreds of related stories to tell; some have merit, some have no merit, and we could write another 10,000 pages about the assassination and still not know any more than we do now. If another tragedy, such as the assassination of our President on November 22, 1963, should ever occur again, god forbid, we must not let history repeat itself. We need to let the investigation of President Kennedy's death be a blueprint of what not to do. Now you know why we will never know the full truth about the assassination of President John F. Kennedy

Assassination Records Review Board
600 E Street NW • 2nd Floor • Washington, DC 20530
(202) 724-0088 • Fax: (202) 724-0457

December 1, 1997

Mr. James Tague
2719 Ellis Court
Plano, Texas 75075

Dear Mr. Tague:

Thank you for taking the time to meet with me on Friday, November 21, 1997, to discuss the work of the Review Board. It was very interesting to hear your first hand account of the events that occurred in Dallas on November 22, 1963, as well as subsequent events.

I hope you will keep in mind the mandate of the Review Board to make the historical record of the assassination as complete as possible for the American public. If there are any records that you think of that should be in the JFK Collection at the National Archives, I would appreciate hearing any thoughts you have on this subject.

Again, thank you for meeting with me. Please do not hesitate to contact me if you have any comments, questions or suggestions regarding the Review Board's work.

Sincerely,

Thomas E. Samoluk

Thomas E. Samoluk
Deputy Director

Printed in the United States
16989LVS00001B/83